the mystery of 23
GOD SPEAKS

KELLY M. WILLIAMS

ELECTIO PUBLISHING
first century principles.
a twenty-first century approach.

The Mystery of 23: God Speaks
By Kelly M. Williams

Copyright 2018 by Kelly M. Williams. All rights reserved.

ISBN-13: 978-1-63213-530-8
Published by eLectio Publishing, LLC
Little Elm, Texas

http://www.eLectioPublishing.com
Printed in the United States of America.

5 4 3 2 1 eLP 22 21 20 19 18

The eLectio Publishing creative team is comprised of: Kaitlyn Campbell, Emily Certain, Lori Draft, Jim Eccles, Sheldon James, and Christine LePorte.

Publisher's Note
The publisher does not have any control over and does not assume any responsibility for author or third-party websites or their content.

DEDICATION

To my Momma, Linda Sue Williams
R.I.P.
(October 7, 1946–March 6, 1992)

Your life was cut short. You taught me to listen to His voice
and ALWAYS do what He says, regardless of the outcome.

I hope my life has honored your legacy well.

Thank you for always believing in the call of God on my life.

And second...

To all those who have heard God and did what He said without
seeing the outcome you had hoped for so far in life . . .

"The voice of the Lord is powerful; the voice of the Lord is full of majesty"
(Psalm 29:4).

Keep listening, keep obeying, and keep believing what you do
for God matters, and in the end, that is *all* that matters.

ENDORSEMENTS

"Often the most impactful insights come to us from outside our comfort zones. Like me, Kelly Williams was not raised in a tradition where God seems to speak to us audibly or through visions. So, the way the Lord speaks to Pastor Williams is a fascinating element of *The Mystery of 23*, as are many of the behind-the-scenes details of one of the noisiest scandals in the recent history of the church. But if that's all you get from this dramatic story, you will have missed the point. Kelly reveals all this with a pastor's heart, a heart that loves and reveres the Word of God and references it often. That is where the true treasure lies here. The rest may intrigue and even shock you, but the emphasis on how God speaks to us through Scripture could change your life."

—Jerry B. Jenkins, Novelist & Biographer,
Author of 192 books, 21 *New York Times* bestsellers,
with more than 70 million copies sold, JerryJenkins.com

"The book that you are holding is a fascinating one. Kelly has masterfully woven together his own story, his walk with Jesus, cultural events, and astute biblical reflection into a beautiful journey that you will be grateful to have undertaken. With unexpected turns, this journey will bring you closer and deeper to God's divine revelation—exactly where you want to be."

—Daniel Fusco, Pastor, Crossroads Community Church,
Author of *Upward, Inward, Outward and Honestly*

"Pastor Williams highlights how one megachurch dealt with their leader and founder's personal indiscretions. I met Kelly through this series of unfortunate events and challenges in 2006. There are powerful lessons here for *all* organizations, both sacred and secular, who are faced with scandalous behavior from their top executives. This book will give you the courage to do the right thing, regardless of the outcome."

—John Weiss, Chair, *Colorado Springs Independent,* *Colorado Springs Business Journal* **&** *Pikes Peak Bulletin* **(over 140,000 weekly readership)**

"Kelly Williams is a man of true integrity, character and faith. These godly traits along with his leadership, patience, and spiritual steadfastness have given him a platform to share an amazing story of diligence and courage. *The Mystery of 23* is intriguing yet inspiring. Weaved in this personal story is the experience of dealing with a ministry dilemma that became a crisis both personally and spiritually. The vagaries of humanity are never-ending, as is the heart to find resolution. The challenge for any authentic spiritual leader is, *What shall I do, and how should I do it?* The journey of life is never about doing the *good thing* but always doing the *right thing*. How difficult this is when doing the *right thing* comes with fear, potential retaliation, and spiritual isolation. But God has a resolution to every untenable situation. In this book's situation, Kelly could have done the good thing, that is, just prayed about it and hoped things worked out. But instead he did the right thing. There was a confrontation that ultimately ended in a sin exposed. Doing the right thing took more time, but the Lord always vindicates and gives grace. In this book, don't miss the one important thing: God's grace will always see you through. The number *23* might not mean much to you, but after reading this book, you might see something incredibly divine in it."

—Michael A. Ware, Founding Pastor, Victory Church

"I first met Kelly and his wife, Tosha, in 1996 when we were apartment neighbors. My perception of them was, *Just a couple of kids launching out into a new and risky ministry*. That was when their church was pure vision without form and structure. Today, Kelly and the church he planted have grown into something much more substantial and influential. As Kelly's church plant began to grow and flourish, we developed a deep mutual respect and warm friendship. Kelly became a man I admire and trust. My friend and fellow pastor,

Kelly Williams, has developed from a competent and accurate handler of God's Word to one who actively and attentively listens for His direction every day. I have seen him respond in faithful obedience to the Lord's direction. He shares in this book how the servant of God can both follow the precepts of the Word and experience the intimacy of *personal* words from the Lord. Kelly doesn't impulsively say, "God told me . . ." Rather, he tests every word that is given to him by the measure of the Scriptures. He has given me the courage to step into similar experiences and to expect God to speak in those times when we need specific direction from our Lord. His passion, discipline, and devotion to biblical integrity have been instructive and exemplary to me. I am confident they will likewise be helpful to the reader."

—Armin Sommer, Senior Pastor, Grace Church on the Mount

"I have known Kelly Williams for around ten years, but I had no idea how engrossed I would become in this book and how in virtually every chapter I would not only feel his frustrations and pain but I would also see myself reflected in his attempts to make sense out of things that made no sense—yet knowing, like the author, that God would ultimately make sense of all things, even when we are the central character to the confusion. Saul and David both messed up as anointed kings in Israel, yet only David acknowledged his sin and repented of it, while Saul stubbornly refused to do so. This book is not about condemnation but is about encouraging us to pursue redemption even if it's through our flawed faithfulness, knowing that ultimately God will make all things beautiful in their time (Ecclesiastes 3:11)."

—Jack McKee, Senior Pastor, New Life City Church

"Karl Barth once said that 'God may speak to us through Russian Communism, a flute concerto, a blossoming shrub, or a dead dog.' In *The Mystery of 23*, it's a number. Echoing Barth, Kelly Williams not only reminds us that God speaks in ways that don't always align with our rational sensibilities, but we ignore this divine voice at our own peril. Drawing from his own personal encounter with the inexplicable, Williams dares to share his story even with those he knows might be weirded out by his Jim Carey-like fascination with all things *23*. Along the way, he does more than simply encourage readers to develop ears to hear God's still, small voice. He also demonstrates what it looks like to have the courage to respond. I highly recommend it."

—Dr. Kutter Callaway, Professor of Theology and Culture, Fuller Seminary, Author of *Scoring Transcendence, Watching TV Religiously,* **and** *Breaking the Marriage Idol*

"I read the book and believe it will serve to warn pastors and church goers so that what happened here doesn't happen again."

—Coleman Jarrell, Former Pastor

"During the season when Pastor Kelly received the vision from God he describes in this book, I was the chair elder at Kelly's church. To his credit, I believe Kelly was transparent with his journey and submitted to our direction as his elder board every step of the way. He admits that the events he shares in this book made him feel "crazy"—and rightfully so because it is a wild story. But I believe the story is true. I am a witness to much of it. Kelly and I have remained close friends through the years, so I have been honored to walk with him through the humiliation, confusion, and torment he has endured. Yet Kelly's scars will not be in vain; nothing is wasted in God's economy. I believe that Kelly's motivation for sharing this story is coming from a good place. Kelly's story gives me hope that during the crazy seasons of life, the divine never abandons us. The great "engine of the universe" is good, and in time, all our difficult stories will be redeemed and used for glory."

—Vance Brown, CEO, The National Cybersecurity Center, Executive Chairman, Cherwell Software

"There are certain places in the world where it seems that heaven quite literally meets the earth. Many places in Jerusalem feel that way. We stood in a narrow corridor, on the ancient stones lining the Via Dolorosa, and Kelly shared something with me that was on his heart. I could sense his angst, but his story sounded quite strange. As he spoke, the descending sun was casting long shadows through the Old City. A random number caught my eye directly above Kelly's head on this wall that was around to witness Jesus' slow march to the cross. The number was *23*. I blinked and stared at it, waiting for the sun to stop playing its tricks on me. But there it stood, a clear and undeniable sign that our God is bigger than we can imagine. His ways are not our ways. There are certain times in our lives where it seems that God quite literally speaks directly to us. This story is one of those times. I knew that Kelly had wrestled with a direct intervention from our Lord, but he never elaborated to me the depth of this encounter. Until reading this book, I never realized this struggle had been going on for so long, preceding the events that went public so many years later. I cannot fathom the turmoil Kelly went through in being dutiful to God's direct call to confront and admonish a peer. This could have been a beautiful story of redemption, but instead it is a warning to all of us that forces of good and forces of evil are continually warring, and as believers, we are eligible to be drafted into service at any moment. Perhaps after reading this, more of us will be like Kelly, bold enough to answer when we are called and deserving of consideration as a 'good and faithful servant.'"

—LTC (Ret.) Jeff Tiegs, US Army Special Operations, Soldier, Servant, Abolitionist

"I am excited to recommend this important story to all who cherish their spiritual journey of hearing from God and obeying His voice. Kelly has been a fellow pastor who, years ago, planted a church near the church I pastored at the time. I have respected his integrity in ministry and in our friendship. Kelly's story and the honesty with which he tells it will grip your heart. Anyone who has ever struggled through understanding what 'hearing God speak to them' means will identify with Kelly's journey and will profit from the lessons from God that Kelly shares with a humility anchored in biblical truths. I pastored through that 'spiritual 9-11' too and am amazed by how God has blessed His church with grace and peace through this spiritual attack. Kelly's public leadership has been a key part of this grace and peace. In this account, you and I learn of how God used Kelly's obedience behind the scenes. This will give you hope that staying faithful, over time, is worth the sacrifice. God is faithful."

—Alan W. Scott, Trinity Church of the Nazarene

"Having walked with my pastor through many of the hard days and sleepless nights that birthed the narrative of this book, I can tell you that every breath of it is real. The 'gift' of prophecy is all sunshine and roses when you get to share good news. But the moment God burdens a human heart with the weight of His holiness? That's when so-called faith is either strengthened or squandered. We believers are all called to deliver God's words with great care—and how much more so when every rational-thinking counselor advises to cut and run. Kelly Williams never cut, and he never ran. The words you'll read in this book are the fruit of his courageous obedience. They may also be the catalyst you need to choose faith in the face of fear."

—Richie Fike, Worship Pastor, McKinney Church

"It is God's nature to reveal, and Kelly's book is about a man who listens to God and moves out in obedience with the result often not being what we anticipated. I have known Kelly for twenty years, and his 'learning to hear' and 'recognize' the Lord's voice has dominated his life and ministry. I write each word with the sincere belief this is genuinely who Kelly is."

—Priscilla Sparks, Retired Navigator, Wife of the Late Doug Sparks

"For Pastor Kelly Williams, the number *23* is not just synonymous with basketball's legendary Michael Jordan, soccer's David Beckham, or baseball's great Don Mattingly. The number *23* has become a vivid reminder of God's faithfulness to countless generations and to his very own life and ministry. I had the distinct pleasure of walking with Kelly through much of the accounts recalled in *The Mystery of 23,* and I can honestly say that Kelly is one of the few men I know who walks the walk that he talks. And because Kelly walks alongside the Father, you can trust that what he says about discerning God's voice and will. I am confident you will be challenged, and your faith

will be uplifted by the many personal stories and anecdotes shared in *The Mystery of 23*—so much so that making sense of the swirling world around you won't bring you stress but will take you to the very feet of the Father."
—Brian A. Beatty, Senior Director of Worship, Media & Hospitality, Vineyard Cincinnati Church

"To say the least, it has been interesting, having a front row seat to the unfolding story as Kelly managed the challenges of obedience in the face of strong resistance. Whether you agree or disagree with Kelly, you would be hard-pressed to dispute his sincerity. Sometimes sharing truth is as natural as eating or sleeping. At other times, the truth can be hard to hear and even more challenging to communicate. I'm grateful for Kelly's willingness to speak out when silence would be the easy path—the more common choice. Knowing Kelly for many years, I've come to expect a direct approach from a man who seldom pulls his punches. He often speaks truth into my life, and I have learned to trust him as a faithful friend. It is my hope that Kelly's candor will ultimately be an encouragement to you. I have been the beneficiary of his truth speaking many times over many years."
—John Pauls, Senior Pastor, Austin Bluffs Community Church

ACKNOWLEDGMENTS

We have some dreams from when we were children of doing things for God; other things, well, they are thrust upon us in the night when we least expect it. This story falls into the latter category.

I never dreamed that I would find myself in the midst of such a grueling ordeal and that I would find God in a way I never anticipated. The journey of bringing this book into existence has been nothing short of a miracle from God. Even as I hit *send* on the final manuscript of this book, fear rests mightily upon me.

I know when this book goes forth it could have little to no affect—or worse, it could have the wrong affect. I have sought counsel, wept, rewritten, prayed, begged, and pleaded for signs and counsel from my seven layers of accountability. I believe to the best of my ability I have sought the Lord and His counsel for my life regarding this book. But I guess some things must go forth and take on a life of their own before you can know, fully know. The life of faith is just that, a life of faith.

I want to thank the following people for believing in the message of this book, but more importantly, for believing in me and the calling that God thrust upon me one morning at 1:23 a.m. These people kept my "crazy" intact. Without you, I would have already quit, I know it:

Vance Brown: for standing with me all those years ago as the elder representative on one of the hardest days of my life. Thank you for guiding me all those years and keeping me from acting and responding out of lesser motives than I believe I am now. John Pauls: for being not just a good friend but a great friend and allowing me to vent my fears and concerns. Thank you for speaking life and truth into me when I didn't know what to do. Armin Sommer: for allowing God to use your life in a way you never anticipated and letting me selfishly have my "own personal counselor," speaking God's Word and truth to me and helping get me through the very dark and uncertain times of what to do. Thanks for being Balaam's donkey when I needed to hear from God and couldn't. Jon Elsberry: for graciously listening to my cries and complaints and then taking those to God every Tuesday and asking God to give us the next step. To the numerous elders at the church I pastor as well as other pastors who stood with me and fought for the message of this book when I wasn't sure it was worth fighting for. To my Life Group 50 men: for speaking life into me along the way. To all those who were willing to risk themselves and endorse this book with nothing to gain in return: thank you! To my church family who said, "We believe in you." Thank you! To my sister, who "gets" the whole prophetic, "I think God said . . ." scenarios of life.

To my five kids who have walked this *crazy* journey. Thank you, Anastasha, Christianna, Joshua, Annalarie, and Journey Grace for helping me see and find *23s* when I needed them. I am forever grateful for your belief in me as your Dad and spiritual guide.

To my beloved bride, Tosha, of twenty-five years when this book is finally published. You have walked every step of the way through these past seventeen years, and I know it has taken its toll on you. Thank you for courageously standing with me. We have no idea what this book will cost us, but we decided *together* it was worth it. Thank you, my love, my Fair One!

To my blessed Savior, Jesus Christ. I have no idea why You chose me for this mission and used such bizarre means to reveal Yourself to me. I will never look at a *23* the same again. For every time I see "23," Lord, I think of You and I hear You say to me in my head and heart, "I see you, Kelly. I am with you, Kelly," and most importantly, "I am *for* you, Kelly." Thank You, Jesus!

And last, I want to thank you, the reader. I know you could be doing a million things with your time other than reading this book. Thank you for investing in this bizarre story. I hope it proves profitable for your eternal heritage. And just maybe it will help someone fulfill their God-given calling in this life. Blessings!

Contents

FOREWORD

This is the story of two pastors from opposite ends of the evangelical spectrum. The author, Reverend Kelly Williams, may be viewed as your garden-variety, Baptist-rooted, Dallas Theological Seminary-trained church planter. The tender shoot he and his wife and friends carefully planted and nurtured more than twenty years ago was seeker-oriented and drew a largely young, single audience. Today it is a multiple-campus church.

The other pastor—whom Williams refers to only as his "friend" and "the man"—had founded his own church in his home in the early 1980s and had seen it explode from a small gathering to a megachurch of many thousands, to become one of the most influential churches in the United States.

An independent church, it was charismatic/Pentecostal based, and it was not unusual for its parishioners to experience visions, visitations from God, and miracles. That's why the vision in the wee hours that eventually triggered this book is so surprising. It did not come to the charismatic pastor. Rather, the troubling, horrifying vision came to Pastor Williams.

It began a seemingly endless trial from which Kelly wished God had spared him. He had been shown the sins of his friend—which would not come to light for six years. For all that time, Pastor Williams felt the weight of that terrible knowledge and suffered the consequences of trying to reveal it. He loved his friend and wanted to help him, but it seemed his every effort backfired, and he was made the villain.

But this is more than a story of vindication when salacious allegations finally proved true. This book is as valuable for its Bible-centeredness and the lessons Williams learned through the ordeal.

As his recurring vision seemed to always wake him at 1:23 in the morning, and other life events appeared connected to the number *23*, Kelly began to wonder whether there was anything to the so-called "23 enigma." The supposition of significance in that number is usually attributed to the superstitious. But then visions are usually attributed to one faction of the church too.

Impressed by the story, I felt compelled to tell Kelly that my birthday is on the 23rd, as is my wedding anniversary. And I had recently experienced a bizarre coincidence in which my son was assigned to room 623 in a hospital and I to room 623 in a nearby hotel. I confess I find such things only interesting, but you might feel differently after reading this book.

Kelly Williams's friend's dramatic fall from grace was as widely covered as any national news story, and the scandalous nature of it gave it even more life. While Kelly prayed the truth would come to light and justice would be served, he never wished his friend ill. He wished him healing.

This is a sad, sad story, but you'll be warmed by Pastor Williams's honesty and transparency, and if you're like me, you'll resonate with his approach to church work and evangelism too.

Somehow this difficult story refreshes, and you'll be glad you read it.

—Jerry B. Jenkins
Novelist & Biographer, Owner, The Jerry Jenkins Writers Guild,
JerryJenkins.com

WHY DID YOU PUBLISH THE 23 BOOK?

The story that frames the background of the 23 book began officially in 2001. God awoke me and asked me to do something that if I would have known at the time what it was going to cost me, I may have joined Jonah in running the opposite direction. However, as God does with all of us, He spoon-fed me incrementally the calling that He placed in my life at 1:23 am on an early February morning in 2001.

As you read the book, the story spans from 2001 and culminates in 2006. Those five plus years—almost six—I was consumed by the "Lord did you really say this to me?" syndrome. I doubted everything I could about me, God, His church, and just about everything else about my life. I felt like I was losing my mind, my faith, my courage, and even at times my will to live. Nothing seemed to make sense to me, and certainly, God was at the most confusing epicenter of my experiences. I was angry, afraid, confused, anxious, and consumed by the question, "God, why did you pick me?" Over time that question turned into, "God did you really pick me or did I just make all this up in my head to make myself feel like I matter to you and your kingdom?"

When the truth finally came out in 2006, I was "happy" that I had heard from God, but what kind of person is "happy" that another person had fallen publicly as the man did in my story? What kind of demented vengeance seeking person had I become? Over the next almost decade, I limped along doing what God asked me to do while in the back of mind and mostly in my heart struggling with the question, "God, what was the point?"

My new friend, "the man," didn't repent. I did everything I could to try and get him to realize that repentance was the best option and direction that he should go. However, in the end, he chose not to listen, to walk away from accountability, and even come after me to ruin my reputation. For a decade I mulled over the point of the story, and why God called me to run toward the burning building, knowing full well I wouldn't be able to rescue him from the years of choices he had made to bring him to this point.

I fretted, I tried to make sense of it, but then I just gave up. What I found happening in my heart was that I was slowly dying inside. My passion for doing what God asked of me waned and I felt the fire of my commitment to Him dying. I guess you could say, "I kept serving God faithfully on the outside, but on the inside, I was no longer sure any of this really mattered." It is still hard for me to admit such an unfaithful attitude when the Lord Jesus had done so much for me.

I felt if I was going to overcome the darkness that was eclipsing the light of my faith, I was going to have to put in writing what I had experienced in hopes of making sense of it for myself and getting some relief and direction for the future in light of my past dealings with the man. If I did not take the time to put this in writing, I was not sure I could continue to use the gift of prophecy God entrusted to me. My calling was on the line; I knew I needed to get free from the misery that nothing I did for God mattered.

So, I wrote it out. As I rekindled my memory with my journals, the emotion was so high I had to write in increments little by little, similar to how God revealed his truth to me in this situation. Over what seemed like an eternity, I finally committed it to paper. For the first time, I didn't have to use my memory or heart to keep up with the feelings and thoughts I felt as a result of my experiences. I could finally rest in the fact that it was written and I could come back to it as often as I needed to try and get a sense of how to release it to God and move on.

As I wrestled through the emotions and thoughts from my past, God began to show me that His ways are not my ways and His thoughts are not my thoughts. He began to reveal to me that His plans are never thwarted as in the story of Job. He showed me that He was in charge all along and He knew what the outcome would be. Then I wondered out loud, "Lord, then why all the pain for seemingly no repentance or good purpose?"

Slowly, God began to show me that His holiness matters to Him, even if it doesn't matter to us, his leaders, or even His church. Just as He did with Jeremiah, He calls us to stand against the lethargy of the day and declare the truth of who He is even if everyone else shouts, "Be quiet!"

However, that wasn't all God wanted to reveal. He also began to show me that the story that "the man" and his wife shared publicly was not unlike the story of Ahab, Jezebel, and Naboth. Ahab and Jezebel fabricated a story when they stole Naboth's vineyard and killed Naboth, and the situation prompted the prophet Elijah to stand against the evil of the day, so the nation of Israel would realize God's truth and holiness matter to God even when it doesn't matter to anyone else, leadership included.

God showed me that whether or not the man repented, His holiness mattered to Him and He expected it to matter to others who claimed the name of Jesus. I watched the man reject my help. I watched him choose to deny what he had once confessed as true and walk away. It turns out I wasn't the only one tormented during the period from 2001-2006. The man's lack of repentance led him to seek out other means to fulfill the sinful pleasures of his flesh, and on the day of reckoning, an unbelieving gay prostitute was used by God to do what he wouldn't allow the church to do. I was reminded of this simple truth that we repeatedly see in Scripture. When the church doesn't address the sin in its camps, God uses the world to hold the church leadership accountable. God did this often with the nation of Israel in the Old Testament. When Israel wouldn't listen, He would raise up one of the pagan nations like the Chaldeans during the time of Habakkuk in chapter 1:

> *⁵ "Look among the nations, and see; wonder*
> *and be astounded.*
> *For I am doing a work in your days*
> *that you would not believe if told.*
> *⁶ For behold, I am raising up the Chaldeans,*
> *that bitter and hasty nation,*
> *who march through the breadth of the earth,*
> *to seize dwellings not their own.*

⁷They are dreaded and fearsome;
their justice and dignity go forth from themselves.

⁸Their horses are swifter than leopards,
more fierce than the evening wolves;
their horsemen press proudly on.
Their horsemen come from afar;
they fly like an eagle swift to devour.

⁹They all come for violence,
all their faces forward.
They gather captives like sand.

¹⁰At kings they scoff,
and at rulers they laugh.
They laugh at every fortress,
for they pile up earth and take it.

¹¹Then they sweep by like the wind and go on,
guilty men, whose own might is their god!"

Habakkuk's Second Complaint

¹²Are you not from everlasting,
O LORD my God, my Holy One?
We shall not die.
O LORD, you have ordained them as a judgment,
and you, O Rock, have established them for reproof.

¹³You who are of purer eyes than to see evil
and cannot look at wrong,
why do you idly look at traitors
and remain silent when the wicked swallows up
the man more righteous than he?

¹⁴You make mankind like the fish of the sea, like
crawling things that have no ruler.

¹⁵He brings all of them up with a hook;
he drags them out with his net;
he gathers them in his dragnet;
so he rejoices and is glad.

16Therefore he sacrifices to his net and
makes offerings to his dragnet;
for by them he lives in luxury,
and his food is rich.

17Is he then to keep on emptying his net
and mercilessly killing nations forever?

Eventually, God uses the world to judge the church when the church refuses to address sin in its camp. God is holy, and He expects us not to be perfect but to be holy. To respect holiness is to believe that God demands repentance. If we do not offer repentance for our sin, He brings judgment.

I wanted my new friend to repent. I wanted a happy story. I wanted to see tangible evidence that the suffering I had endured at the hands of this vision had come to fruition and brought about redemption. That was not to be the case. It is hard to imagine that God gets glory out of unrepentant people, but the Bible teaches that God will receive glory through both the unrepentant and the repentant. We see this in Romans 9:

14What shall we say then? Is there injustice on God's part? By no means! 15For he says to Moses, "I will have mercy on whom I have mercy, and I will have compassion on whom I have compassion." 16So then it depends not on human will or exertion, but on God, who has mercy. 17For the Scripture says to Pharaoh, "For this very purpose I have raised you up, that I might show my power in you, and that my name might be proclaimed in all the earth." 18So then he has mercy on whomever he wills, and he hardens whomever he wills.

Moses was repentant. Pharaoh was not.

God shows mercy to the repentant believer, and He shows wrath to the unrepentant. Either way, His power is made known, and where God's power is revealed, His glory is established.

The story of my friend shows God's longsuffering nature. His desire is for all to repent; it is what the Scriptures teach us. However, we have a choice. We can walk away. Moreover, though my friend wants to paint a story that no one tried to help him, I have learned that I am one of many that went to help him. God is a patient God, and He has seemingly endless compassion for His people. However, eventually, He brings judgment, and He will use the world if the church isn't faithful to do the work of Jesus. It is a hard pill to swallow, but one I have now accepted.

As painful as this journey has been for me, I accept that whether my new friend has repented—or ever repents—God's glory is revealed. If God's people repent, His mercy is on display, and He receives the glory. If we don't repent, His wrath is poured out, and He gets the glory. It is God's way.

As I began to settle this in my heart, I have discovered as people read this story, I wasn't the only one who had done hard things for God and hadn't seen the result they wanted. My story began to give others hope and getting to hear how God eventually brought the truth to light gave others hope. Moreover, as my story began to restore hope in others who read it, it restored hope in me that God receives the glory regardless of the outcome.

I wonder how many people out there have given up on God because they stood against the sin of an influential person who claimed the name of Jesus and they were eaten alive for it. They haven't seen the resolution I have seen. They haven't had the opportunity to see it play out on such a public stage. Also, because of this, they are may have lost hope and are giving up on doing what God has asked of them. Their faith is diminished, and they need a reminder that God's holiness matters above all else, and He will eventually get the glory one way or the other. They need to hear, "What you did for God STILL matters. God sees you. God is with you. God is STILL FOR you."

Because I saw how this was helping others and myself, I felt prompted to contact publishers and see if this was a story that could potentially help others whom I had never met or may never meet. What dark corners of the world are people hunkered down wondering if the risks they have taken to expose sin and welcome people into repentance was worth it?

This story is the ring God asked me to carry and yes, like Frodo, I have said, and I am sure I will say again before it is all said and done, "I wish this ring would have never come to me." Then I hear those wise words from Gandalf, "So do ALL who live to see such times, but that is not for them to decide. All we have to decide is what to do with the time that was given to us."

I didn't choose this; it chose me. However, now I must see it through for the glory of Jesus. I must carry this ring to "Mordor," so to speak. Sadly, many have tried to silence my voice in publishing this book. I cannot assume anything about another human's motives, but I do know what God has asked me to do for the church, and this book is a huge part of it. I must see this through. I am unable to say that I want to publish this book. I am unable to say that I need to publish this book. What I now know is this: if I want to be obedient to God, I HAD to publish this book if I was going to be obedient to the original 1:23 am prompting.

It is my hope this book can be used to encourage you to do what God has asked of you, and restore accountability in His church.

It is my prayer that the reoccurring symbol of 23, now a redemptive reminder for me, will become a symbol that will launch a revival in the heart of God's prophets, not unlike Elijah standing against Ahab one day and wishing for death the next day. It is recorded in 1 Kings 19:

¹Ahab told Jezebel all that Elijah had done, and how he had killed all the prophets with the sword. ²Then Jezebel sent a messenger to Elijah, saying, "So may the gods do to me and more also, if I do not make your life as the life of one of them by this time tomorrow." ³Then he was afraid, and he arose and ran for his life and came to Beersheba, which belongs to Judah, and left his servant there.

⁴But he himself went a day's journey into the wilderness and came and sat down under a broom tree. And he asked that he might die, saying, "It is enough; now, O LORD, take away my life, for I am no better than my fathers." ⁵And he lay down and slept under a broom tree. And behold, an angel touched him and said to him, "Arise and eat." ⁶And he looked, and behold, there was at his head a cake baked on hot stones and a jar of water. And he ate and drank and lay down again. ⁷And the angel of the LORD came again a second time and touched him and said, "Arise and eat, for the journey is too great for you." ⁸And he arose and ate and drank, and went in the strength of that food forty days and forty nights to Horeb, the mount of God.

The LORD Speaks to Elijah:

⁹There he came to a cave and lodged in it. And behold, the word of the LORD came to him, and he said to him, "What are you doing here, Elijah?" ¹⁰He said, "I have been very jealous for the LORD, the God of hosts. For the people of Israel have forsaken your covenant, thrown down your altars, and killed your prophets with the sword, and I, even I only, am left, and they seek my life, to take it away." ¹¹And he said, "Go out and stand on the mount before the LORD." And behold, the LORD passed by, and a great and strong wind tore the mountains and broke in pieces the rocks before the LORD, but the LORD was not in the wind. And after the wind an earthquake, but the LORD was not in the earthquake. ¹²And after the earthquake a fire, but the LORD was not in the fire. And after the fire the sound of a low whisper. ¹³And when Elijah heard it, he wrapped his face in his cloak and went out and stood at the entrance of the cave. And behold, there came a voice to him and said, "What are you doing here, Elijah?" ¹⁴He said, "I have been very jealous for the LORD, the God of hosts. For the people of Israel have forsaken your covenant, thrown down your altars, and killed your prophets with the sword, and I, even I only, am left, and they seek my life, to take it away." ¹⁵And the LORD said to him, "Go, return on your way to the wilderness of Damascus. And when you arrive, you shall anoint Hazael to be king over Syria. ¹⁶And Jehu the son of Nimshi you shall anoint to be king over Israel, and Elisha the son of Shaphat of Abel-meholah you shall anoint to be prophet in your place. ¹⁷And the one who escapes from the sword of Hazael shall Jehu put to death, and the one who escapes from the sword of Jehu shall Elisha put to death. ¹⁸Yet I will leave seven thousand in Israel, all the knees that have not bowed to Baal, and every mouth that has not kissed him."

It is my prayer that my story will remind the "Elijahs" of the world that they are NOT the only ones standing for the holiness of God regardless of what it costs them. Instead, God has (so to speak) 7000 more prophets who refuse to bow the knee and kiss the hand of Satan in hopes of experiencing the "success" of the church today especially in America. It is my prayer that this book prompts the church of God to listen to the prophets of God, so that the Lord doesn't have to raise up the pagan world to judge them. Either way, God will receive the glory.

God, use us for Your glory REGARDLESS of the outcome and may we not fear the consequences of being used by You. Instead, let us anticipate the crowning glory we will receive when we hear you say, "Well done my good and faithful servant."

I am glad God didn't reveal to me all that He would require of me when this journey began. However, I can say now looking back over the past 17 years, I am glad to have served my Lord in such a way. I consider all that I have lost along the way as worth the glory my Savior has received through the truth of His Word being triumphant, even if it isn't the "happy" ending I desired when I set out on this journey.

I am reminded of the words of the ancient prophet Samuel when Saul sacrificed "for" God, but was disobedient in his actions. Saul had the spirit of religion, but had lost his real relationship with God. Samuel says to him, "Obedience is better than sacrifice." What was Samuel saying to Saul? Possibly he was saying, "What I have given up for God can never excuse me from my responsibility to simply do what He has told me to do." I pray this is the same for you as we each bear upon our bodies the marks that show our surrender to Him. May you be inspired to do whatever God asks of you. Know that, along the way, the outcome will bring glory to God, regardless of what it is. God's glory is ALL that matters.

Say with me, "Speak, God, and we will obey for your glory regardless of the outcome!"

It's 1:23 am.

INTRODUCTION

I t began at 1:23 a.m.

Something or possibly someone awakened me out of a deep sleep. I sat straight up in my bed, sensing a presence in my room. My wife lay in the bed next to me, asleep. Wide awake and confused, I began to see what I would now call a vision. My room was dark with a bit of light from the street. The red numbers—1:23 a.m.—on the alarm clock glared at me from my right, but my mind's eye was drawn to the light of this vision. I saw someone. Within this vision, I sensed God's displeasure for *this person.*

I began to sense and see things that were a part of another's private life. I was overwhelmed by the emotion of the scenes that I saw.

Probably like you, I have had many "bad" dreams in my lifetime. I could fill books with stories that I have seen in my sleep and worries that have come out of the dreams of my sleep. However, this was different—really different. I was freaked out.

As quickly as the vision came, it left. My body was tingling with fear, anxiety, worry, concern, and just a deep sense of, *What the heck just happened to me?*

Having grown up a Southern Baptist pastor's son in Kentucky, I had seen and experienced a few things in my lifetime that had more than freaked me out and left me with little explanation of what just happened to me and those around me.

As a young evangelical, I was taught to "walk by faith" but figure out a rational explanation ASAP. I'm a Southern Baptist, a graduate of Jerry Falwell's Liberty University, and a graduate of Dallas Theological Seminary with a master's in theology. This resume in hand, my mind went to work fast to solve this dilemma with a "that makes sense" sort of answer.

I said to myself, *This couldn't be real, could it?* I learned a long time ago that, when something goes "boom" in the night, it is either God or gas. I got up to eliminate the one about which I could do something. On my way back to bed, I tried to shake off what I had just experienced, but I was spooked to say the least.

I said to myself, *What just happened to me?* I lay back down in bed, facing my wife. She was still sound asleep. It seemed like an eternity but as I looked at the clock, only a few minutes had passed. Little did I know that this moment would monopolize the next *sixteen years of my life* and bring some of the greatest pain and humiliation my life has ever experienced, setting me on a journey that I am still trying to make sense of today.

Perhaps you, too, are on a journey with God that you are trying to make sense of. How do we discern God's voice in our lives so we can make sense in our everyday, routine, boring, who cares kind of lives?

That is the big question. Really, the simpler question is, Does God speak to us personally? Does He talk to us? Does He use things and people to speak into our lives individually, and, if so, how? Beginning that night at 1:23 a.m., I began to learn more than ever before how He does this.

I don't expect you to believe everything you will read in this book. For years, my hesitation in writing this has been my overwhelming fear of hurting someone and being left to look like a fool in the process. I don't *understand* everything that I am going to share with you, but I can assure you, it happened, I was there, and I am still trying to make complete sense of it.

But I also know that God was in it.

As a Southern Baptist pastor of twenty-plus years, I have learned God uses a variety of ways and methods to communicate with human beings. One of the most common ways He uses to convey His will is through *visions* and *dreams*. These words occur 198 times in the Bible. Proverbs 29:18 even says, "Where there is no prophetic vision the people cast off restraint." But do these things still occur today? Joel 2:28 says, "And it shall come to pass afterwards [in the last days]. . . . your sons and your daughters shall prophesy, your old men shall dream dreams and your young men shall see visions." This same sentiment is repeated in the New Testament in Acts 2:17-21.

This reality scares me, but it is the epic of the One True God of the Holy Bible.

When I was nineteen years old and a freshman at Liberty University, I met my future wife, Tosha. She had been a journaler since she was thirteen years old. Through our developing friendship and dating relationship, she challenged me to take up journaling as well. So, in the summer of my nineteenth year, I began putting my thoughts on paper—something I have continued to this day. This exercise would provide invaluable data for me to recall and write the content of this experience that spanned over a half decade of my life.

I am confident that you will either be really encouraged by what you are going to read, or you will toss this book aside and declare me a kook. Just so you know, I wouldn't blame you at all. I have wondered and wandered through this process and often thought, *I'm losing my mind. It is crazy of me to even take the time to write this down.*

One of my favorite seminary professors used to say, "Men, you know the difference between those in the insane asylum and us? We on the outside have learned to manage our crazy." Well, at times I am not sure I have done a very good job of "managing my crazy," and after you read this, you might agree.

Now at this point I am not sure what image it is that you have of me. Do you see me like Albert Einstein with wild hair, odd glasses, and bizarre ideas? Can you envision me as the "Doc" in the *Back to the Future* movies with a lab coat and crazy hair? Maybe you envision me as a creeper with a pale face and sinister eyes.

Whatever image you have of me, I am probably different than what you might think. I am a plain, simple country guy who happens to be a pastor. I graduated from high school with a 2.7 grade point average. I got cut from my high school basketball team multiple times. I grew up on a dairy farm in Kentucky and spent more time with cows than people as a kid. These days, a good day to me is when I hang out with my family and our black angus cattle down in the barnyard. You may say to yourself, *Well, that explains it!*

Oh, that the ways God speaks to us were as easy to explain!

The Mystery of 23, which began that night at 1:23 a.m., haunts me, compels me, inspires me, scares me, frees me, and invites me to experience how, though I cannot yet fully explain how it works, the divine speaks into my everyday, routine, boring, who cares kind of life.

It is important for you to know this book is not a book about how numerology fits with biblical interpretation through numbers, though numbers played a very significant role in my "vision." The number *23,* for whatever reason, is the number God chose for me; your experience will more than likely be different. However, I am learning how to hear God speak in ways that I never, ever saw coming through this experience.

I invite you to join me on this journey of discerning God's voice for your life too. Because who we are and what we do for God matters. It matters to God. And in the end, it is all that matters.

Section 1:
The Beginning

9 + 11 + 2 + 0 + 0 + 1 = 23

I don't know if you have ever heard of the phenomenon known as the "enigma of the number *23*." Throughout time, people have been enamored with this number. It has proven to carry great "coincidence" with a lot of major national, political, scientific, and astronomical phenomenon. Sports stars love to sport it. Our bodies are made up of 23 pairs of chromosomes. The tilt of the earth's axis is 23 degrees. It takes a drop of blood 23 seconds to circulate through a human's body. The average human physical biorhythm is 23 days. There are 2,300 stones comprising the Great Pyramid. The number *23* is the lowest prime number that consists of consecutive digits. Primes have been described as the "atoms" of mathematics.

John Nash, the Nobel Prize-winning economist who was the subject of the film, "A Beautiful Mind," was obsessed with *23*. He published 23 scientific articles. The most detailed account of the assassination of Julius Caesar, written by Nicolaus of Damascus, claims numerous enemies stabbed the Roman emperor 23 times. William Shakespeare was born on April 23rd and died on April 23rd. William Wallace was executed on August 23rd.

The first Morse code transmission—"What hath God wrought?"—was from the Bible passage Numbers 23:23. The 23rd verse of the first chapter of Genesis brings the act of creation to a close while the 23rd chapter of the book of Genesis deals entirely with death. The 23rd Psalm is the most popular psalm. Psalms is the 23rd book of the Bible, there are 23 letters in the Hebrew alphabet, and "W" is the 23rd letter in the alphabet. (I wondered why I was named "Williams." Ha!) The list could go on and on and on and on. Just google it if you don't believe me. The number *23* is a phenomenon that is curious and unexplainable.

In the summer of 2001, something awakened me at 1:23 a.m. nearly every morning. The number *23* quickly became a fixation of my imagination until it became a routine bore to my existence as I continued to wake up at 1:23 a.m.

With each sleep interruption, I became more and more bored with the "phenomenon" taking place in my head, my heart, my thoughts, and emotions. I don't know what it is like to be an alcoholic, a porn addict, or a drug addict, but I assume that at some point the high becomes the norm and eventually "using" is normal. At some point in this journey I came to expect my sleep to be interrupted in the night. It became the norm. As a matter of fact, I was even surprised when I slept through the entire night. I wondered in those moments what was wrong.

I jotted down Scriptures, conversations, thoughts, feelings, and slowly trekked toward the fine line between crazy and crazier. With each new person I introduced this bewildering exercise to, I was becoming used to the divine "using" me.

I take annual breaks every year, and so I took my annual break that summer of 2001. In the midst of that break, the divine bug bit my wife. She started having dreams and feelings, thoughts, and images of women with sons and no husbands. She assumed because of the bizarre experiences I was undergoing that she would get pregnant with a son, and then I would soon afterward die, and she would be forced to raise him alone.

This fear turned into terror. She dreaded the nighttime. She was becoming equally paralyzed by the divine. While she was preoccupied with the fear of me dying and leaving her to raise a family alone, she began to sense that it had more to do with others than us. She saw the way this experience was affecting me, and she knew it was a big deal. She equally began to feel that something big and bad and involved lots of moms raising sons without fathers was going to occur.

While Tosha was being overwhelmed with grief from a tragedy that had not occurred yet, I decided that I couldn't take it anymore and that I had to probe the natural to see if the divine, the supernatural, was for real. During my break in the summer of 2001, I started pushing into the *facts* of the vision I had received. I wanted to see if what I had been experiencing behind closed doors in the dark of night at 1:23 a.m. was God or gas. Pardon my irreverence, but to me it all boils down to the natural or the supernatural, one or the other.

I reached out to my new friend . . . and I heard these words from the Lord:

His message is for me, but his heart is FAR from me.

What was I to do with that?

With each moment I would become exhilarated that maybe I had cracked the code and figured out the divine only to sink quickly into the mire of complete fear and agitation, wondering, *Why did God pick me for this?*

All of us will be chosen by the divine for tasks in this life that leave us baffled by why He chose us. We can accept our mission, or we can fight it, but we can't change it.

In the Bible, there are only two people who had visions and dreams and could interpret them as well. They were Joseph and Daniel. Ironically enough, both of them were punished for this ability. Joseph had a dream in Genesis 37. It says in Genesis 37:5, "Now Joseph had a dream, and when he told it to his brothers they hated him even more."

Joseph naïvely shared his vision of how God wanted him to be faithful to serve Him and his family. However, his family hated him for it. Whenever God uses visions or dreams to reveal His will for us, inevitably our naïve obedience leads us into unexpected negative repercussions. Both Joseph and Daniel ended up in prison because of their willingness to follow God and do what He told them to do through visions and dreams. This was true for Joseph, Daniel, and myself, and I hate to tell you this, but it will be true of you as well.

I pressed on amidst the angst, often frustrated by more moments than not. I tried to quit, but *23* just kept haunting me. I was beginning to be able to see the images of the vision whenever I would close my eyes to go to sleep. It was pressing on me like I was being driven down an alley like a herd of cows or a group of common criminals being led to the execution line. My gut tightened often with the anxiety of what lie ahead, and my heart often raced with anticipation of what lie just beyond the dark alley. I was in the midst of the greatest divine moment of my life, and I couldn't understand any of it.

The summer finally came to a close and my break ended, and I was able to go back to work. I was never so glad to be able to have something to focus on. I thought I could share my dream/vision with a few people, and like a bad dream, they would tell me there was nothing to it and I could go back to doing my thing.

It felt like a prison was closing in around me, and my choices were becoming limited—even removed—from my own will. I had chosen to listen to God. I had chosen to respond to God. I had chosen to not argue with God, and now I was being given a mission I didn't know how to fulfill for God. I needed relief.

I had borrowed a CD from a friend that summer. I love worship music. (I know worship is supposed to be the "warm-up" for the senior pastor's message, but I *love* worship.) It was the latest anthems by Passion. These anthems would later become my saving grace and the battle cry for me to move forward. Even to this day, I can't listen to this music without it conjuring up in me the emotions I felt that summer and fall of 2001 as I wrestled with the divine shadows in that dark alley.

I remember the words of one song: "Shout to the east and the west, sing to the north and south, Jesus, the Savior to all, He's Lord of Heaven and Earth." These words along with many of the words on that CD brought great hope, peace, and comfort to my soul as I sensed the divine preparing me for a battle, a battle I didn't think I could win, a battle I didn't know how to fight, a battle that would prove harder in the end than I could even imagine.

As the haunts of the divine cornered me now day and night, I was coming to terms with the fact that my will had to be a part of this equation. I had to stop fighting, guessing, doubting, and start claiming that greater was He who was in me than He who was in the world. I had to declare that we wrestle not against flesh and blood but against principalities and powers in the darkness. I had to accept the "ring" that had been placed around my neck and carry it whether I wanted to or not. At times it fascinated me, at other times I felt special because I had been "chosen," but honestly, most of the time I felt crazy, confused, and down-right mad that I had to be the "sucker" for the mission.

But at some point, like me, if you feel this way about what God has placed in your life to do, I have learned that you have to decide to stop asking why it happened and start asking, *What should I do since it happened?*

Finally, I decided I had gathered all the "spiritual" intel I could gather by comparing the natural to the supernatural. I had shared with a couple of my elders along with a couple of my staff members, and I was setting in motion a plan to try to naturally discern if, supernaturally, the divine had called my number.

Although I had yet to meet him face to face, I scheduled a lunch with my new friend.

In the midst of this transitional holding pattern before we had lunch, 9/11/2001 (or *23*) took place. Since 9/11 many have looked at the numbers of the date of 9/11/2001 and added them up to $9 + 11 + 2 + 1 = 23$. Just google it. I won't argue the accuracy of this way of adding up the numbers of dates, but what I will say that God used "the coincidence" in my life and seemed to parallel this great tragedy with the challenges He seemingly had set before me.

The horror of this devastation haunted us, our community, our nation, and yes, I think even our world. The world had changed, the Cold War had given way to the new era of terrorists using our airplanes to devastate our way of life.

The aftermath and images of 9/11/2001 or the United States of America's *23* was greater than words can describe. The two buildings that symbolized financial prosperity were gone, and with it, thousands of souls.

The natural met the supernatural on 9/11/2001 (*23*) and from our perspective it was devastating. This was the start of a long, painful battle our nation would face This time looking back would equally prove to be the beginning of a long, painful personal battle I would be called to fight in the spiritual realm.

The number *23* had struck us both, and the devastation was unimaginable.

THE MORNING AFTER

There are experiences in our lives that happen in one day and shape the rest of our days.

How many times did we all watch and re-watch the video footage and images of the Twin Towers falling in New York City after that dreadful day? In just a few minutes, the history of our entire nation was irrevocably altered with the falling of the Twin Towers and the death of almost three thousand souls on that grave day. Ash chased souls down the streets of New York City as they sprinted to survive what seemed to be the end of the world.

I remember it was Tuesday. It was my regular sermon-writing day. It was a beautiful sunny morning. I kissed my wife and two little girls goodbye and headed to the office to begin my regular routine of fasting for the day and writing a sermon for our church's weekend services.

While I was seated at my desk in my office, writing, Tosha, my wife, called and said, "You need to turn on the radio or get to a television, an airplane has hit the Twin Towers." The feeling of complete confusion, fear, anxiety, and panic rushed over me. I couldn't get to a television, so I pulled it up on my radio. The first tower had already fallen, and the second tower was on fire. The chaos was at a complete frenzy, and no one at the time knew exactly what had just taken place.

We later learned the horrific details of a group of terrorists that had highjacked four planes and were planning to use two of them to fly into the World Trade Center, one into the Pentagon, and a fourth into the White House itself. Thankfully, due to the courage of the passengers on Flight 93, the plane that was bound for the White House was intentionally crashed in a Pennsylvania cornfield before it could reach its destination.

Since that day, our nation has never been the same.

There are experiences in our lives that will occur that will shape the rest of our existence. 9/11 is one of those days for our nation.

Amid all this national chaos, my wife and I were dealing with this "23 mystery." Certainly nothing in comparison to the images and losses we saw on the television the day after 9/11. I remember Tosha and I standing for days, weeks, and even months after 9/11 and staring at the television during the evening news as story after story emerged from this devastation and atrocity that had been wreaked on our nation. Somehow your mind was telling you, *If I stare at this long enough, I will either wake up from this bad dream or some sense will come from digging deeper and deeper into this saga our nation has endured.*

Yet, sometimes, the longer you stare at things, the more real they become and the less they make sense to the mind and especially to the heart.

The vision that I initially experienced occurred in February of 2001, just seven months prior to the worst catastrophe our nation has experienced probably since Pearl Harbor on December 7, 1941.

In the midst of this national trauma, our nation was at war, and we didn't know who or where our enemy was.

For the duration of the year, I had found myself in a war, and I didn't know who the enemy was or where to find him. My life went from simple to daily panic attacks that kept me up at night paranoid by the sounds and sights of the night. My anxiety grew with each dream; each time I was awakened by this "presence." It became almost comical to be awakened. I finally reached the point to where I stopped looking at the clock because I already knew, it was 1:23 a.m.

No longer did I ask myself, *Is it God or gas?* Something or someone had my attention. I realized that I needed to start recording my experiences and capture my thoughts on paper. Somewhere between February and August of 2001 my vision experiences morphed into journaling sessions where I asked and begged the Lord for Scripture to confirm that I was not crazy, and if I was, to know what to do about it.

I cried. I hadn't cried, really cried, since my mom was killed by a drunk driver in 1992. It had been a decade of numbness and complete wonder as to whether God had seen. Did He care? Even if He did, did I care anymore? *I was a church planter who secretly hated God.* It is a tough combination when you have to preach every week about the "love" of God.

I confided in my wife that I was having these "visions" and that I was getting up in the night now and writing in my journal, trying to make sense of what to do next. She encouraged me to talk to my pastor friend. I began sharing with him about my visions, but I learned that I had a very hard time sharing with anyone. Every time I talked about it, it made me *very* afraid. It gave me panic attacks and caused my hands and feet to sweat profusely, leaving me confused, dazed, and down-right angry at times. I couldn't control how it made me feel, and so I tried, tried, and tried not to talk about it. But I couldn't; when I remained silent about it, it made me feel even more crazy. The urge to tell someone, anyone, everything I knew was overwhelming, but how do I tell someone I had this vision in the night at 1:23 about a man I didn't know? I can assure you that if you approached me with this, even if you were my closest friend, I would recommend a sleep aid or some therapy or memorize a few more Scriptures and call me in the morning.

Like those images on the screen the day after 9/11, the longer I looked at them made no difference. I couldn't make sense of these visions or even come to terms with them. All of us have moments like this in our lives where something happens to us or someone we love, and we can't make sense of it. We have divine experiences that rationale cannot explain. We have moments in which we know *something* or *someone* visited us, but we can't put it in words. We felt the presence, we felt the effects of the presence, but the mind is saying, *That never happened*, while the heart is saying, *What just happened?*

In 2001 it didn't matter how often I wrote about the vision or how often I shared it with my wife, close friends, and spiritual authority; I was haunted by it. And even though I was haunted by it, like the images I saw on that screen the day after 9/11, I said to myself, *This can't be real, this can't be happening.* But it was, and it did.

In counseling, therapists call this post-traumatic stress disorder, or PTSD, where your body goes through a trauma it can't process and so it shuts down until it has the capacity to process the elements involved in a devastation of this magnitude. For some people, they never recover; for others like myself and maybe you, we walk with a limp, confused and dazed by what we have experienced.

But like those images on the day after 9/11, at some point, we have to live again. At some point, we have to say, *I don't understand what has happened to me, but I was there, it happened. I saw it with my own two eyes. I experienced it with all the senses that God has entrusted to me. Yes, I am confused. Yes, I am completely baffled by what I know to be true from my experience. But whether or not I gain the meaning of "why," I can't let go of the truth that I know to be true despite the pain that accompanied it.* For this real experience that occurred in your life, whatever "it" is for you, I am here to do what I and our nation needed someone to do for all of us in 2001. I am here to say to you, *What you have experienced is real.*

You and I don't have to keep staring at our experiences to authenticate them or to convince ourselves they occurred in order to be able to figure out why they occurred. I have learned through this you have to *keep acknowledging the spiritual experiences happened, even if you don't yet understand why they happened.* You are not crazy. You need to stop staring into the past and say to yourself in the mirror tonight before you go to bed, "Whether anyone else believes me, I am a spiritual being, and the Divine knows my name. I know what I experienced was from the Divine, and I accept it as equally if not more real than the bed I will sleep in tonight."

ONE NATION

T he debate over whether to take the name of God out of the nation's pledge of allegiance ended, and our nation turned its full attention toward a war that needed our prayers as we sent our sons and daughters off to find an enemy that couldn't be identified and wouldn't fully be identified for over a decade to come.

My wife's vision of her bearing a child and me dying soon after unfortunately bore light right before our eyes as special episodes of news shows would feature young women whose husbands were lost on 9/11, either because they were going about their daily lives of work in the building or they had been called upon by our country to risk their lives to save the lives of their fellow Americans. Many paid the ultimate sacrifice that day, and story after story would offer up pictures of these young women who were now widowed, expecting sons on the way. Although it wasn't *me* dying, the feelings from the vision were real.

Tosha just sat and wept and wept and wept. She would say to herself, *God, why did You tell me this ahead of time? I couldn't do anything about it. Why?* She wept even more as no answers came and the tension of trying to understand only grew with each question, each episode on the television screen. Helplessness was common, and fear was rampant, even out of control in all of our lives in the daily task of trying to make sense of such hatred and devastation.

In the midst of this devastation of young moms losing their husbands while expecting babies, many of which were sons, we learned that we were expecting our third child. We had two beautiful little girls, Anastasha and Christianna. Now we were expecting our third. Would this strange 1:23 a.m. vision eventually claim my life like 9/11 and leave Tosha single, expecting a son like so many others on that day? We feared it. We prayed against it. We didn't know what lie ahead, but we knew the "bad" was no respecter of persons, and if my mom being killed by a drunk driver had taught me anything, it had taught me that death comes when you least expect it and devastates the fabric of your existence beyond measure. We, at least I, had learned to live expecting the other shoe to drop. It's a terrible way to live but nonetheless the often residual effect of losing someone you love dearly at a very early age.

Without fail, we had watched Tosha's divine encounter play out on the television screen, and now we were left to wonder if it would play out personally in our lives now. Would my vision cost me my life?

As God continued to visit me at 1:23 a.m., I was starting to learn the lesson that *a spiritual experience eventually requires a physical response.* Heaven collides with earth, and the battle becomes now three dimensional and real in a way it never was before. I sensed that I was supposed to do something with the things God was revealing to me. I needed to talk to my friend, but I was scared.

The promptings of God at 1:23 a.m. were haunting me. Every time I saw this number I was tortured. What do I do with what I have experienced? Everyone eventually has to do something with what they have experienced, either pretend it didn't happen or respond to it and see how you can help. It can be anything from giving money to someone else, to helping someone with their marriage or an addiction, to risking and attempting to adopt a child. Regardless, eventually a spiritual experience requires a physical response. Or as I heard someone say recently, the miraculous demands motion.

Try as I might to ignore the promptings, I couldn't any longer. I followed through with my lunch appointment.

I regretted scheduling the lunch meeting. Fear was rampant in our hearts. What would happen next?

I went to the lunch appointment. I arrived first. I prefer this, as it gives me a chance to get my bearings, get situated, and try and deal with some of my nervous energy before my new friend arrived.

He arrived and greeted me. "Hey, good looking." Due to the nature of the vision, his comments made me very uncomfortable. I brushed it off as a joke and welcomed his presence.

We had a wonderful time. I had never had lunch with someone that I felt I had more in common with than this man. I resonated with the way he thought and the way he processed life. I admired some of his observations about life and the divine. We had a wonderful time, but I walked away from that meeting with the resounding reminder that this was not about friendship; it was about trying to discover how the divine had orchestrated me as the one to try and help in this situation. I had to set aside my personal thoughts and compare it to my divine encounters to discern what it is that I was supposed to say, do, or not say or do.

With each of these mile markers along the way down this dark alley, I feel like the Divine would momentarily turn on a street light and let me catch my breath and bearings only to shoot out the light and send me once again back down the alley with little to no knowledge of what the point was or how it would eventually play itself out in the end. Fear was my companion.

In that meeting I told him that I had visited his church service that summer. Then we talked theology, the nation, and the importance of God in our nation at the time of such great national crisis. We were two men under God in a nation that was desperate for God. Billy Graham was able to share the gospel with our nation multiple times during this time period, and people really seemed to be *one nation under God.*

Though the trials were massive, the peace and unity of a nation under God was beautiful to experience as well at the same time.

Our lunch meeting neither confirmed nor denied my vision, it just helped me to get to know him in a natural setting since the supernatural is the only place I had ever met him.

My respite from the emotional angst was short lived, and soon the divine shadows in that dark alley came calling again. This time it was a Tuesday. I was fasting and writing my sermon. I knew it was time. I could deny it no longer. I called one of my staff members and then a couple of my elders and then I proceeded to call "the man."

I have to do something, I thought to myself, *and I have to do it today. I can't carry the weight of this any longer.*

I called him and he answered. I told him that I would like to meet with him about something that was heavy on my heart. I indicated it was of a personal nature and requested a meeting where we could talk in private.

I wasn't sure how he would respond. And if he did agree to meet with me, I wondered how long it would take to work through our schedules and meeting logistics. I felt a heavy burden to get this done, and I expected delays. But to my surprise, he readily agreed to meet. But there was an odd twist.

Even with the twist, I was relieved. I worked though my schedule and adjusted my plans so I could accommodate our meeting. I talked with my accountability team and with my wife. It seemed surreal, but it was finally going to happen. Before long, all the logistics had fallen into place, and I had a green light from my accountability team and my wife, despite the unusual nature of the meeting.

Still, looking back, I am not sure why I was so willing to accommodate "the man's" unusual twist. But I was, and when the time came, I followed through and made the trip with my journals in hand.

October 16, 2001

I feel very burdened this morning. I told Tosha last night that I believe the Lord wants me to confront him. I am very nervous, and I feel very weak. The past two days I have felt very burdened and vulnerable. Oh God, may You speak to me through Your Word and give me wisdom in how to handle this situation. I have placed two calls to him in the last weeks and have yet to hear back from him. Speak to me, Lord, and tell me what to do. I will do it.

In my devotions today the Lord spoke to me about him through Numbers 17–24. The chapters deal with Balaam confronting Israel. Balak wanted to curse Israel, but God wanted Balaam to bless Israel. God told Balaam to go but say what He tells him to say. In chapter 24 he no longer consults divination. Instead, he turned and looked out toward the wilderness, where he saw the people of Israel camped, tribe by tribe. Then the Spirit of God came upon him, and this is the prophecy he delivered . . .[1]

My time has come to confront him.

I called his cell phone and got his voicemail with his assistant's voice on it. He changed it in the last two days. I called his main office and got his assistant. She put me straight through to him. I told him I needed to talk to him as soon as possible. I told him I wanted to talk in private. We agreed on a meeting in the parking lot of a Wal-Mart. I have called my wife, my chair elder, and my good friend Doug (an older gentleman who was a retired Navigator. He has since gone to be with the Lord.)

D-day has arrived. In a few hours I will either have one of the biggest messes on my hands or I will be the biggest fool to live. I would be willing to be a fool if it meant avoiding the other, but my heart tells me that "the man" has fallen and now it is my desire to make a commitment to him and his family to love them and help them the next two years as they struggle through this. Lord, give me the grace and wisdom to love "the man" deeply.

God gave me another powerful confirmation, maybe the greatest yet. God tells Balaam through His own prophecy, you, who hears the words of God, who has knowledge from the Most High, who sees a vision from the Almighty, who falls down with eyes wide open:

Give me courage, Lord, and compassion to speak what You have revealed to me.

---

1.   This is a direct quote from my journal. I don't record what the Bible said about Balaam's vision.

After completing my journey and arriving by car at the designated Wal-Mart parking lot, "the man" was nowhere to be seen. I wondered briefly if this was some kind of joke. But only a couple of minutes later "the man" pulled up in a car beside mine. He had a big grin on his face as he rolled down his window and said, "Did you bring the drugs?" That caught me off guard, but I assumed he was making light of meeting in a parking lot. Still, it reminded me that this was anything but a routine meeting.

He said to me, "Why don't you get in my car and we can talk." I got my journals and got in his car.

Our nation was just weeks removed from maybe the greatest tragedy we have ever faced as a nation, but like me and my new friend, we were bewildered and befuddled but still *one nation under God.*

What would happen to our nation, to him, to me? I had no idea, I was just trusting God, like our nation was, that I was under His authority regardless of the outcome. I just knew at this time this *reoccurring spiritual experience from God demanded a physical response, and I was going to obey, regardless.*

CHURCH STREET NEAR DISASTER

A number of years after 9/11, my family and I went on a road trip to the east coast. For years the city and nation did not know what they would do with the area that had become known as Ground Zero since 9/11.

When we visited in 2009, they were building a Freedom Tower in honor of the lives lost that day. Even though the wreckage of 9/11 was long gone, the feelings and the sense of sorrow remained with the murals and flowers that lined the streets and the area around Ground Zero. I was surprised to realize that the Twin Towers were on "Church Street." That was strange to me. Just across the street and down a ways was an old church building that turned out to be the first Catholic church ever built in New York City. I don't ever remember the media mentioning any of this.

On the day of the attack, scores of people ran down Church Street toward the oldest Catholic church standing in New York City to flee the debris that was swirling, mushrooming, and consuming out of sight the presence of scores of people. What a picture of people running to the Savior. What a picture of people realizing this world is not their home. What a picture of two mighty towers that hovered over the city, now gone, but a little white church remained as a place of protection, cover, and hope.

When I got in that car with him I can now say I felt like that little white church that had been ignored by scores of others to head to the Big Towers. However, on that day, I hoped that I could be a place of refuge for him to run to, in order to avoid the mushrooming cloud of destruction that was becoming his life.

On October 20, 2001, I recorded this in my journal as a follow up to the meeting I had with "the man."

October 20, 2001

I want to return to 10/16/2001 and record my time with him. I met with him in a Wal-Mart parking lot. We talked for two hours. I began by sharing how I had struggled with a desire to have an affair the last two years. I shared how this past May the Lord freed me from the bondage. I no longer feel that stronghold over my life.

I then turned to my journal and said, "now I want to share something from my journals, and if I be wrong, would you please show mercy upon me?"

I read him four entries. I mostly looked down at the page, and he mostly stared out the window into space with very little to no emotion. I finished and closed my eyes and wept a few tears. He asked me if I was OK. I told him, "I am very burdened and heavy for you.""

For the next hour or so he showed no response. He confided some past struggles and told me he has maybe 3 or 4 reasons why he may be disqualified. I ask what they were, but he would not tell me until he talks to his wife. He asked me a couple of times what I thought he should do. I told him that I don't even know what he has done, but I sense the Lord saying, "Step down now."

I told him I wanted to make a two-year commitment to him to get him help and restoration. He asked me to pray for him, I told him

I have and will. He said, "NO, I mean lay hands on me and pray for me now." So I did.

I asked him when we would talk again, he said, "In a week or so." I told him this is too serious to let go indefinitely. He told me to call him Tuesday (10/30/2001). He would be in Detroit but could talk over cell phone.

Ever since I have had many emotions. The following morning I had this overwhelming sense that he was suicidal and could easily kill himself. I felt that for two days. I also sensed he could kill me. But since Friday morning, I have sensed he is going to come clean. Lord, may You strengthen me under this burden. May You help me to love and serve "this man" as You desire. Give him the courage to address and deal with this issue in a way that is pleasing to You.

When I got out of his car he said to me, "Are you going to be OK?" I said, "I don't understand." He said, "What do you not understand?" I said, "I have just confronted you about a very serious issue, and you have admitted to having a problem and have disqualified yourself in three or four ways, and you seem to be OK with it." He said, "I learned a long time ago that God doesn't need me, and if I don't fulfill what He has called me to do, He will just get someone else." (I don't agree with this by the way.)

There I was, standing outside his car. His life was crumbling all around him like the World Trade Center towers. He had a choice to make like the people who were outside the towers. He could run for Church Street and find strength, hope, and freedom, or he could stay in that car and let the debris from the attacks of his life bury him alive.

The church on Church Street may not be as impressive as the towering Twin Towers, but neither was the destruction around it. Looking back now over a decade later through the eyes of having since visited Ground Zero, I have learned from God through this experience that *it is our responsibility to try and be a redemptive presence in other's lives, regardless of how painful the world around us may be or whether they accept our help.* Our redemptive presence matters. However, unfortunately as our naïve obedience to Christ wears thin, it is easy to lose sight of this mandate. But we must not give up on reaching out to our friends, family, and neighbors and trying to help them with the crisis of their lives, especially when God puts something on our hearts to share with them.

I longed on that day and the days to follow that he would choose Church Street and run for that little white church to escape the swirling, mushrooming, out-of-control destruction that had become his real life.

The choice was his.

You have people you have reached out to because God has put them on your heart. And just like the people on 9/11, they can see you, the little white church, as they run from the debris of their lives that falls all around them. But like my friend, they have a choice.

All we can do is try to be the little white church and help them.

The choice is theirs.

THE SPIRIT OF SAUL OR DAVID

W hen I sat in the car with my new friend, he said to me, "I think I am Saul." I had no idea what he meant by this comment, so I asked, "What do you mean?" He said, "I used to think I was David and that I had God's favor on my life, but anymore I feel like King Saul, and God has taken His Spirit and His favor from me."

It is the same way our nation felt after 9/11. We are a nation founded on Christian principles. Our Founding Fathers each took time to seek the Lord. Alexander Hamilton even attended that little white church on Church Street in New York City in the 1700s. Our history is rich with Christianity, with Jesus Christ being our cornerstone. Since 9/11 many have felt that the hand of God's blessing has been removed from our nation, and we are in a fast leak toward the end of time.

Whether you are a nation of Christian principles or a Christian person, the thought of God removing His hand from you and taking His favor from you is a very scary thought.

I remember when I attended Dallas Theological Seminary in Dallas, Texas. One of my professors would say to us in Christian leadership class, "Men, do you know what scares me the most as a follower of Christ and leader for God?" He would pause—we all wanted to know. Then he would say, "That God would remove His hand of blessing from my life and take His Spirit from me."

I have never forgotten that statement, and when my new friend said to me, "I feel like King Saul, and God has taken His Spirit and His favor from me." It took me right back to my seminary days. When 9/11 occurred, it took all of us back. If we are honest, we all wondered, *Is this it? Is God done with us as a nation?*

My new friend wondered this, our nation wondered this in the days that followed 9/11, and Saul wondered this. If we are honest, we all wonder at times, *Is God done with us? Are our best days behind us?* It's a horrible thing to ask and an even more horrible thing to consider. It's terrifying.

I said to him, "You don't have to be King Saul. King David blew it, but he turned to God and repented of his sin, and God forgave him. You can be David! You can have the Spirit of David on your life, not the spirit of Saul." This is true for all of us. All of us are under the blessing of forgiveness if we will simply ask. Our sins, mistakes, shortcomings, and failures do not have to be the end of our story. They can be a new beginning where God redeems, restores, and rebuilds you to be the man or woman He has created you to be. Yes, we may walk with a limp after that, and we may entertain regret because of our perfectionist pride, but in the end, *God is for you and me.* He is for us succeeding in this life and more importantly in the life to come.

Lamentations 3:33 (NLT) says, "For he [God] does *not* enjoy hurting people or causing them sorrow" (emphasis added). God is for you. Regardless of what you have done wrong, God is for you, but He can't act in your life if you refuse to repent. We have to choose either the Spirit of Saul or the Spirit of David. God doesn't give us either. We have to choose it. We have to choose to be a rebellious person or to repent. We have to decide who and what matters the most to us—and then act.

First Samuel 28 records part of the story of Saul. Saul had gone ahead earlier and made a sacrifice without the prophet Samuel. He was king, and though he was first in charge, he had made the mistake of thinking that *first in charge* meant *in charge of everything.* It's a common mistake all leaders are tempted to make, especially when you are the point leader of an organization. No one is able to lead in a healthy manner over a long period of time without accountability. You learn that accountability is not for punishment but for protection.

Saul, for whatever reason, didn't understand this principle. He thought if he were king he could simply do whatever he wanted. But as we all learn, and so did Saul, being king doesn't make you God. It just makes you king.

Saul violated the holy codes of God. He consulted the divine at his leisure and in his own way, and this cost Saul greatly. It cost him the Spirit of God, and it cost him the favor of God.

After Saul repeatedly refused to be led by the voice of God through him, eventually Samuel came to him and said, "The Lord has torn the kingdom of Israel from you this day and has given it to a neighbor of yours, who is better than you" (1 Samuel 15:28-30). At this moment, Saul reveals who he had really become.

The years of disobedience had clouded his judgment, and instead of turning and repenting, he simply asked Samuel the prophet to come back with him so the people would at least think he was still the king and seemingly still had the favor of God on his life. Samuel obliged, but God was done with the game of charades.

Saul became so desperate that he consulted a medium. I see this ancient phenomenon playing out today in scores of Christians who have given up on being able to hear from the divine. They are tired of trying to understand the mysteries of God and decoding the divine messages and missions that God has for their lives. They are finished with waiting on God for understanding. They are tired of thinking, *God will come through some day.* They are taking matters into their own hands and resorting to the worship of crystals, seeking advice from fortune tellers, calling psychic hotlines, reading their horoscope, and the list of deviants goes on and on and on. They, like Saul, are desperate—but not desperate enough to repent because somehow, some way, they see this as God's fault, not theirs. It is one of the greatest ploys of the enemy: to convince us that God is not for us so he (the enemy) can get us to join his efforts in this fallen world.

Most of us don't think we will do certain things to figure out our lives until we are in the moment. I am sure Saul never thought he would go see a medium after he forbid anyone from consulting a medium—but he did. As my father used to say, sin will take you further than you want to go, keep you longer than you want to stay, and cost you more than you will ever want to pay. If any statement is true, that one is.[2]

First Samuel 28:4-5 sets the stage to show what the spirit of Saul looks like: "The Philistines set up their camp at Shunem, and Saul gathered all the army of Israel and camped at Gilboa. When Saul saw the vast Philistine army, he became frantic with fear."

The *spirit of Saul* is just another way of saying the *spirit of fear*. The Apostle Paul tells us in 2 Timothy 1:7, "For God gave us a spirit not of fear but of power and love and self-control." Saul was frantic and afraid. These are the traits the enemy wants to give us. We all experience them, but what do we do with them? What decisions do we make when we are afraid?

Saul went to the Lord: "He asked the Lord what he should do, but the Lord refused to answer him, either by dreams or by sacred lots or by the prophets" (1 Samuel 28:6).

Now you might think, *He did what he was supposed to.* But he didn't. Saul knew he was disobedient. Saul knew he was no longer the king due to his disobedience. Saul knew that the kingdom had been given to someone else. Instead of repenting of his sin, Saul sought the favor of God to gain the blessing of God.

That is not how the divine works.

We can't go to God to get what we want because we know He can give it to us. We go to God to get what He wants us to have, and God wanted Saul to have repentance. God wanted Saul to let go of the hand of God and embrace the heart of God. God wanted Saul simply to repent.

But Saul wanted everything but a contrite heart, and he proves it in the following actions that he takes: "Saul then said to his advisers, 'Find a woman who is a medium, so I can go and ask her what

---

2. Source unknown.

to do.' His advisers replied, 'There is a medium at Endor.' So Saul disguised himself by wearing ordinary clothing instead of his royal robes. Then he went to the woman's home at night, accompanied by two of his men. 'I have to talk to a man who has died,' he said, 'Will you call up his spirit for me?' (1 Samuel 28:7-8 NLT).

In our modern-day vernacular, we call this "channeling spirits." By the way, it works, but that doesn't mean God is OK with it.

The woman replies to Saul:

"Are you trying to get me killed?" the woman demanded. "You know that Saul has outlawed all the mediums and all who consult the spirits of the dead. Why are you setting a trap for me?" But Saul took an oath in the name of the Lord and promised, "As surely as the Lord lives, nothing bad will happen to you for doing this." Finally, the woman said, "Well, whose spirit do you want me to call up?"

"Call up Samuel," Saul replied. When the woman saw Samuel, she screamed, "You've deceived me! You are Saul!" "Don't be afraid!" the king told her. "What do you see?" "I see a god coming up out of the earth," she said. "What does he look like?" Saul asked. "He is an old man wrapped in a robe, she replied. Saul realized it was Samuel, and he fell to the ground before him. "Why have you disturbed me by calling me back?" Samuel asked Saul. "Because I am in deep trouble," Saul replied. "The Philistines are at war with me, and God has left me and won't reply by prophets or dreams. So I have called for you to tell me what to do."

But Samuel replied, "Why ask me, since the Lord has left you and has become your enemy? The Lord has done just as he said he would. He has torn the kingdom from you and given it to your rival, David. The Lord has done this to you today because you refused to carry out his fierce anger against the Amalekites. What's more, the Lord will hand you and the army of Israel over to the Philistines tomorrow, and you and your sons will be here with me. The Lord will bring down the entire army of Israel in defeat."

Saul fell full length on the ground, paralyzed with fright because of Samuel's words. He was also faint with hunger, for he had eaten nothing all day and all night. (1 Samuel 28:9-20, emphasis added)

A few chapters later this is what happens to Saul . . .

Now the Philistines attacked Israel, and the men of Israel fled before them. Many were slaughtered on the slopes of Mount Gilboa. The Philistines closed in on Saul and his sons, and they killed three of his sons—Jonathan, Abinadab, and Malkishua. The fighting grew very fierce around Saul and the Philistines archers caught up with him and wounded him severely. Saul groaned to his armor bearer, "Take your sword and kill me before these pagan Philistines come to run me through and taunt and torture me." But his armor bearer was afraid and would not do it. So Saul took his sword and fell on it. When his armor bearer realized that Saul was dead, he fell on his own sword and died beside the king. So Saul, his three sons, his armor bearer, and his troops all died together that same day. (1 Samuel 31:1-6)

But it didn't have to end that way.

Saul had a choice, and he chose to ignore the evil of his life. He had a choice to flee the debris that was falling all around him and run, so to speak, for Church Street, but instead of taking cover in the little white church that could have replaced his fear with peace, he chased after the world's means of finding peace, and he used the favor of God to assure them that they would be protected. This cost Saul, his armor bearer, his sons, and scores of other people their lives, because the only thing greater than his fear was his pride, and he refused to repent and accept the fact that he had lost his kingdom forever.

You know the story of David and Bathsheba. David slept with Uriah's wife, Bathsheba, and killed Uriah in order to cover it up and take her as his wife. It cost David greatly for the rest of his life, but in a moment when he was confronted by his sin in 2 Samuel 12:13, look at his response:

Then David confessed to Nathan, "I have sinned against the Lord."

David understood that being king didn't make him God. Yes, if you keep reading the story of David you learn that he suffered greatly for his decision, as do we all. The wages of sin is death in this fallen world, but that does not mean that God does not forgive, and that does not mean that God can't restore. It also does not mean that God is not for you. But if you try and cover up your sin and keep the blessings that come from God's favor in your life, it will cost you more than you can ever imagine.

As my dad used to say to me, "Sin will take you further than you want to go, keep you longer than you want to stay, and cost you more than you want to pay."

I prayed earnestly for a week that my new friend wouldn't choose the spirit of Saul but the Spirit of David. But in this season I learned, *redemption is a choice you can't make for others. They have to choose it.*

THE DREAM BECOMES THE NIGHTMARE

It all started at 1:23 a.m. eight months prior to 10/23/2001. The mystery of *23* could take a turn toward redemption, and the divine whispers that had haunted me for over half of a year could begin to see some fruit from them.

The little white church was in sight just down Church Street. Yeah, the debris continued to fall all around, and the fears and anxiety of this life were real and abundant, but I had hope that my new friend would make it to the church and that the mushrooming cloud of debris wouldn't engulf him and leave him for dead on the side of the street with his lungs filled with the destruction of his life.

I was praying new life would be breathed into him and hope would be restored. I was praying this story would have a happy ending and that my labor would not be in vain. I was anxiously anticipating his call. I just knew it was going to be good. Even though the personal devastation was great, there were many unanswered questions, and there was a long road ahead, I believed that, just like God would bring our nation together after horrific events of 9/11, He would work all things in my life for His glory (as recorded in the journal entry below).

On the morning of 10/23/2001, just one zero removed from 1:23 a.m. when this all began, I penned these words in my journal:

October 23, 2001

Today I seek the Lord and prepare a message. It is also the day I am to follow up with "the man" regarding last Tuesday's confrontation. So far I cannot get in touch with him on his cell phone. He is in Detroit at a meeting. I must put together a plan if he does not call me back or I can't get ahold of him. I know he is a very busy man. I pray he sees the importance of calling me back. I will not walk away from this. I must see this through.

Today we go to the doctor to confirm the pregnancy. Tosha is, we think, ten weeks today. We are excited.

I spoke with him. He denied it and did not tell his wife. He said my comments were absurd. He further attacked me. I told him he was a liar and he doesn't have to hide it. I asked him what the three or four things were that he told me last week might disqualify him. He told me today that it was pride, arrogance, competitive spirit, and feeling inferior.

At the beginning of the conversation he attacked me and said I just didn't like his church. He said someone from my church told him I thought his church ministry was sterile, but I told him that—so I am unsure why he would see that as a surprise. I ask him why he did not tell his wife. He responded, "To protect you and save you from looking bad in her eyes."

I ask him why he didn't just tell me last Tuesday that my comments weren't true, his response was he didn't want to hurt me, and he wanted to pray about whether God wanted him to step down. He told me after a week of prayer that God told him not to step down.

He told me I may be catching on to some of his struggles in my prayer time but that he has never done anything to disqualify himself.

I ask him some point-blank questions.

1. *Have you ever kissed a man or woman romantically other than your wife? He answered, "No, though I am close to some people and I do kiss them on the forehead." I said, "Romantically?" He said, "No."*

2. *Have you ever touched another man or woman's sexual parts other than your wife? He responded, "Ever?" I said, "No, since being the senior pastor of the church you pastor presently?" He said, "No."*

3. *Have you ever had a boyfriend or girlfriend while married? He said, "No."*

I then said to him, "I do not believe you." I told him it doesn't have to be this way, but if he doesn't come clean with God, God will remove him from ministry. I told him I wanted to talk to his spiritual authority. He asked me, "Why? Do you have someone who is accusing me of being intimate with them?" I told him I would not answer that question. He pressed me, and I told him again I would not answer.

At this point he gave me a name to call and talk to at his church. He gave me the name of his associate. He gave me his cell number though I later learned he was on the same trip with him in Detroit. He didn't mention that, which would have been an obvious comment to make if he was referring me to someone who was with him.

After he stopped his intimidation and attack toward me, he then began saying nice things about me. He told me he knows my heart is for him and that I care for him. But when he realized I would not back down, he soon dropped this approach. I told him in closing, I give you until tomorrow and then I must take action. He said, "OK" and hung up the phone and that was that.

One other thing, I ask him if I could call his wife and tell her the conversation we had: he absolutely forbid me and said I have no right calling her because I am not his spiritual authority. I told him God had brought me into this and I have a responsibility to see it through. He said, "Well I guess it will be interesting to see how it turns out."

To my utter sadness, he chose the spirit of Saul on 10/23/2001. It grieved me deeply. Soon after this I got a call from the leader of his accountability team.

The voice on the other end of the phone had a deep southern tone to it. Initially the conversation did not go well, but as I began to share my concern, motivation, and aspects of the conversation, I sensed his tone change to concern. I told him that my new friend did not tell his wife like he said he would and did not deny the concerns when first shared—that he attacked me and accused me of being out to get him. I shared that others have confronted him about the possibilities as well. I told him that my new friend confided to me that he was fascinated with homosexuality but had not acted it out and that he confided deep bouts of depression. I told the leader that the thing that stands out the most is that my new friend said he had three or four things that potentially disqualified him, but he needed to talk to his wife first, and he said he would tell me a week later.

After we talked a bit more, the mentor said, "I am calling the local accountability, and we will have a meeting where the members of his board, himself, myself, and someone to be an advocate for me could be present."

Within a few hours, the mentor called me back. He said he would be on a plane, and in two days we would get all this cleared up. My head was spinning. *What had I done? What had I gotten myself into? Why me? Why now? What was about to happen?*

I don't think my new friend expected his mentor to call a meeting. I prayed earnestly that he would feel the heaviness of this and confess and still turn and run to the little white church in surrender. I begged God on my hands and knees for this man to share the darkness of his secrets and get help. I asked the Lord for the grace to love him. I asked the Lord for wisdom on how to show him mercy and grace. I asked the Lord to give me wisdom to know how to speak to these men that were assembling to address this matter.

Throughout all of this, I kept saying to myself, *How did it come to this?*

I began to worry; my mind raced. My crazy had gone to an all-new level of anxiety and fear. I feared my integrity would be attacked, but I kept saying to myself, *I am confident that this is from the Lord.* I wrote this in my journal on that same day:

October 23, 2001

I have no idea how this is going to turn out. I have no idea what is going to happen next. I wonder right now what conversations are taking place. Lord, may You reign supreme in this matter. My faith and trust are in You. I will not fear what man can do to me. I must fear You!

I fear for my new friend for he is going up against You, God, and God, You relinquish Your mercy on us when we don't humble ourselves. God, be merciful upon him. I will not doubt You, God, but I am VERY scared and burdened.

October 24, 2001

Today has been a very, very long day. I spoke to another of his spiritual mentors today. I have a meeting tomorrow at 9:00 a.m. at a hotel. I am very fearful, but I have [been] praying all night and read the book Born for Battle. *It is about spiritual warfare. The book has focused my attention and spoken deeply to me. Give me the grace I need to see this through. I have no idea what will happen tomorrow. May Your will be done, my God.*

October 25, 2001

I go in a couple of hours to meet with my new friend, his wife, and a group of leaders who are over him, and possibly some others. I am very anxious. I have no idea what will happen. Speak to me, Lord, through Your Word. Once again I believe the Lord has spoken to me about this situation with this man and what God thinks of me. In Hannah's prayer in 1 Samuel 2:9-10 she prayed, "He [God] will protect his godly ones . . . No one will succeed by strength alone. Those who fight against the Lord will be broken. He thunders against them from heaven; the Lord judges throughout the earth. He gives mighty strength to his king and he increases the might of his anointed one."

I don't know what Daniel felt like when he went into the lion's den, but I was pretty sure it had to feel something like this.

Unfortunately, the spirit of Saul had been chosen, and I was left to feel the effects of the debris falling all around. The little white church was nowhere to be seen, and the possibility of surrender was gone. The vision of 1:23 a.m. had turned into the nightmare of 10/23/2001; the spirit of Saul was released in his life to take over.

One of the most painful lessons I learned from these 1:23 a.m. encounters with God in this season of naïve obedience is *obedience to God's spiritual promptings in your life to help others may lead to some of the greatest emotional and physical pain of your life.* This pain will cause you to question God, your purpose, and the direction you will take or not take at all in the future when God prompts you to do something again. It is easy to say you will obey God's voice; it's entirely something else to actually follow through and do it—especially the next time.

DIFFICULT HARD BECOMES DIFFICULT DISASTROUS[3]

I have had my fair share of bad days in my life, but the day I met with my new friend's accountability has to rank up there as one of the worst days of my life.

October 25, 2001

Today has been one of the most difficult days of my life.

I thought this day would go very different than it did. I still hoped and thought that the Spirit of David would win out. I still believed there was hope and that "the man" would choose David's Spirit and not Saul's. I was dead wrong, and I have the emotional scars to this day to prove it.

I arrived at the office of one of my elders to meet with him and another elder from our church to pray before meeting with the accountability of "the man." We headed over to the hotel and arrived first, and then the board of four arrived. The board consisted of pastors of other churches and no one from "the man's" church.

3.   Title taken from Bill Hybels, *Leadership Axioms* (Grand Rapids, MI: Zondervan, 2008).

Also, no one outside of "the man" and his wife were present from his church for the meeting.

The meeting took place at a hotel. The board moderator set the tone of the meeting. He asked me to share and then for my new friend to share. I started to open my journals and begin to share, but the moderator asked me not to use my journals but to share from the heart and from memory. So I shared my heart and made myself as vulnerable as possible.

He shared. He twisted, denied, and rebutted everything I said. As I sat there and watched him, I repeatedly asked the Lord if I was wrong, and continually I felt the divine presence saying, *He is lying.* At times he pointed to how important he was because of his ministry. He referred to himself as the pastor of the largest church in the state. Many of his comments were haughty, controlled, and condescending.

The hardest part was listening to his wife talk about how I was wrong, and he was right. I understood. It was her husband. It didn't hurt me most because she was attacking me. I expect the same support from my own wife if I were in that situation. What hurt was watching her innocence and hearing her defend her man while "the man" sat there, letting her do that for him. It is one thing to lie, but is another to deceive your own wife into protecting your lies.

After about an hour and a half, they brought the discussion to a close and asked for closing comments. The board wanted to make this sound like it was a disagreement of opinion. That it was a miscommunication. I said to them in response, "This is not a miscommunication. No less than five times he has lied, twisted, and changed his story. In time the truth will come out—it always does."

In his closing comments he talked down to me and included his wife in saying how *they* hoped this was a learning experience for me and that I would grow through this. They assured me that they had never had anyone address them this way in the long tenure of their ministry, and that even though they were sad that I had done this, hopefully it would benefit me in the long run even at their expense.

At that moment the room was silent, and most people, including myself, wanted to leave. It was the most difficult meeting I have ever been in before in my life. But before we could have a closing prayer, one of the board members spoke up and said, "I suggest to the group that we need to ask Kelly to repent of his accusations."

There I sat, and in the midst of a nightmare that I thought couldn't get any worse, it did. The humiliation that I felt from that statement cannot be described in words. *How could the tables be turned on me? How could it become about me?* That is the enemy's ploy. I can't tell you how many people I know who have been abused in their lives, and the abuser makes the abused feel like it is their fault. This is one of the enemy's age-old weapons that he uses on us, and even though we may know this, the shame and humiliation is beyond words.

On the way out, "the man" said to one of my elders, "Make sure this never happens again," and then he glared at him like he could destroy him in a moment.

That day I recorded this in my journal . . .

October 25, 2001

I went to shake his hand and instead I hugged him—it made him mad when I hugged him and told him I loved him. He backed away from me and peered into my eyes. I saw the demons of hell in his eyes. I saw the hate of hell in his eyes. I saw the lies and the stronghold he has given them over his life. He is a tormented man. He shook my elder's hand and told in a very hushed angry tone, make sure you handle this right next time.

When I walked out of that hotel I thought my insides would explode. I have never felt hell like I felt it today. My innards shook deeply. I felt I would pass out from the weight of the burden and evil I felt I was fighting. I felt naked and very vulnerable.

My elders stood by me. They held my arms up when I couldn't. I could barely make it to the car, and then I fell into the backseat of my elder's car and began to sob, weep, and eventually cry uncontrollably. I hadn't cried like that since my mom died nearly decade earlier.

My elders took me to lunch to feed me. I wasn't hungry. I was numb. It was the same way I felt when I got the news that my mom had been killed by a drunk driver. My heart, emotions, and thoughts were raw with humiliation, shame, and utter embarrassment. I forgot that I don't wrestle against flesh and blood, and I began to struggle with deep resentment toward "the man" immediately. I was a wreck, and I was convinced I would never be able to pastor again.

How could God pick me and then humiliate me like that? How could God ask me to go into the lion's den and NOT close the lion's mouth? How could I be dropped in the desert to do God's will without the power to overcome?

I don't remember much about the next two days. I do remember grabbing the pillows off the couch, turning up the worship music to beyond recognition, and lying on the floor and weeping, weeping, and weeping some more. I was empty, poured out like Paul said—like a drink offering—but for what reason? What good did it do? I had just spent eight months of my life preparing for that moment, and little did I know I still had over half a decade to go before there would be any sense of closure come to that day.

Still to this day, my oldest two daughters, Anastasha and Christianna, remember me lying on that floor. My oldest was four at the time, my second born was two. I remember them saying to their mother, "Why is Daddy crying so much?" Tosha would keep saying to them, "Because his heart is broken."

I had such high hopes that something beautiful would come out of that day. I had such high hopes that righteousness would win the day, and God would triumph victorious over His throne, and the angels would rejoice that one sinner was saved. I had the great expectation that revival was about to break out in the little white church and that the chaos that was falling all around would be gone before we knew it.

I had no idea that day that I would be put on trial for the mysteries of *23* that I couldn't seem to decode with the divine's assistance. I wondered immediately and often if the Lord God who made the universe was truly sovereign or if the prince of darkness had more power. I wondered why I do what I do. Then I wondered, *Did I really hear the divine presence who created me speak to me? Did I make it all up in my head and convince myself of something that just wasn't true?*

This is the universal tension we all feel in trying to hear from God and attempting to discern His voice for our lives. *Maybe I am crazy. Maybe I should quit the ministry. Maybe I should repent. Maybe it is me who has the problem.*

I lay on the floor for hours. I wept for hours. I wept until I couldn't weep anymore. Fear gripped me. I knew my ministry was over. I was a phony. I had lost all credibility. I tried to figure out in my mind as I lay on that floor how I could resign from the church I pastor and move on. I tried to figure out what went wrong, and then it struck me. *I need more evidence.*

The Bible says, "The battle is not ours, it belongs to God" (2 Chronicles 20:15 NLT, paraphrase). It also says, "He fights for those who wait for him" (Isaiah 64:4, paraphrase). Inside of me I had this pull/push battle going on—one minute I knew I needed to get more evidence and nail his backside to the wall, the next minute I knew I needed to resign and go away quietly in hopes that as few people as possible would find out.

As my mind raced, I thought, *Either I need to prove this or quit.* I was wrong about both but too immature at the time to know this. I concluded things in my mind after this and put them in my journal believing they were "thus says the Lord" and God was going to blow this thing wide open in days. Days turned into weeks, weeks turned into months, and months turned into years. I can't tell you how many times I lost hope in this process that the divine would ever make sense to me again, and that is a tall order when you have to preach every week to a group of people.

I was ashamed of myself and felt like I deserved to be punished.

Some of us pride ourselves on pulling ourselves up by our bootstraps and doing what God has asked us to do. The problem with this strategy is, sometimes it doesn't work; it works against us and begins to destroy the work God is doing in us. All of us will face situations in which God has asked us to engage that will lead us to the end of ourselves. When my new friend rejected my help and turned the pain of his life on me, I lost all confidence in my ability to help him or to hear from God.

I learned *the chaos and confusion of the 1:23 a.m. experiences caused me to question EVERYTHING I believed about God and myself.* And I bet it does the same to you. Where do we go from here? Give up?

Thankfully, along the way, like God fed Elijah with the birds in the desert, God sent just what I needed—never more, but certainly what I needed. Thanks to my wife, Tosha, and my executive pastor at the time, I gained the courage to get up off of the floor and preach that weekend at our church. I don't remember what I said, similar to when I preached my mom's funeral. I just did it and hoped that I didn't make a bigger fool of myself than I already had. I didn't do it because I felt worthy, prepared, or like I had something to share. I did it because I was called, and a few who knew me believed in me when I didn't believe in myself anymore.

This was one of my entries during that season.

November 4, 2001

Last night was hard. I didn't want to preach at all, but I did. Help me, Lord, I can't do this without You.

What I have learned over the years is that the Holy Spirit is the game changer. Whatever I can't do, I can do with God.

I look back now, and I see the hand of God's mercy on my life in that season. Like a man stranded on a lifeboat in the middle of the ocean, occasionally a bird flies by and he snatches it out of the air and eats it to stay alive. That is what this season felt like for me. When the water was gone, rain would surprisingly find its way to the canteen of my heart. The Lord would replenish me. He took me back to Lamentations 3 often in that season of my life. The Lord's mercies are new *each* morning, and great is His faithfulness.

About a week or so after the meeting with the board, I got a call from one of the board members. It was the board member who called for my repentance. I had no idea why he wanted to meet with me. I feared it. I couldn't take another beatdown. I couldn't take another attack. My heart was tender, and the brokenness I felt was real.

He asked if he could meet with me in person, so we arranged a meeting.

When the board member arrived, we sat down, exchanged pleasantries, and he said, "I know you were right. I know you were telling the truth, and I am sorry for calling for your repentance."

Tears began to fill my eyes, but confusion began to fill my mind. I said to him, "Why? Why now? And why did you say what you did to me at the meeting that day? It was very hurtful to me."

He said about my new friend, "He is a very intimidating person, and he came to me before the meeting and said to me, 'I need you to have my back. He is planning to go to the newspapers about this.'"

I told this board member I had no intentions of going to the newspapers. He said, "I know that now." He also went ahead to say, "I was in the room with him when you called that day in Detroit along with two other pastors from the church." He said, "That is when he told me that you were going to go to the papers with this stuff if he didn't resign."

As difficult as it was to process the lies and the twisted way in which my new friend had handled the situation, I was relieved to know and somewhat encouraged to hear someone who didn't know me say, "I believe you are telling the truth." It lowered my suspicion of my *crazy factor* a little bit and began to turn the tide ever so slowly to the reality that this was not going to end any time soon.

A few days later I read in my devotions Job 17:9, "The righteous will move onward and forward, and those with pure hearts will become stronger and stronger." I claimed this for my life that day just as Job did thousands of years before in the struggles of his life.

On November 10, 2001, Tosha called me to inform me that my new friend's wife had sent me a six-page letter, stating her thoughts once again on the issue at hand. The packaging of the letter was very bizarre. It was in multiple envelopes. She wrote it to me from a hotel in Dallas and mailed it to the wrong address. It went back to the hotel, and they thought it was their mail and opened it. Somehow they found the right address and wrote me a letter, apologizing for having read it because they thought it was mail to them.

In the letter she was attempting to confront me and let me know how wrong I was and how she hopes I grow in wisdom and allow this humiliating experience to be a lesson to me. She reaffirmed her trust and love for her husband. She expressed how great a relationship they share. She rebuked me with Scripture and told me this was the first time in seventeen and a half years that her husband's board had to entertain an accusation. I found it interesting at the time that she was writing me and not confronting him. I recorded in my journal that day:

November 10, 2001

I am more convinced today than ever. He has hidden it for now, but in time God will make all known. Help me, Lord, to care. Help me not just feel attacked and attack. Help me to trust YOU and to stand on grace. I am the Lord's, and I have done what You have asked me to do. I entrust it to my Heavenly Father and wait for You to speak and move. My hands are tied. I still don't understand, Lord, why You chose me or involved me, but You did, and I entrust it to You. I will not question my God. Help me, Lord, to trust You, and may Your will and power be made known through this very difficult situation. It hurts me to know I have hurt "the man's" wife, and it hurts me that she thinks and feels certain ways toward me. It is hard to bear up under that anger I sense and feel, but I do what my God asks me to do.

Tosha is twelve weeks pregnant. We look forward to May 20th.

On the last day of 2001, I wrote these words:

December 30, 2001

As I look back on 2001, September 11 has proven to be a very monumental day in the life of our country. It has certainly brought to the forefront our weaknesses and vulnerability as a nation, but it has also brought our country somewhat back to God. As I look back over 2001 and the October 25 meeting, I still don't understand the point, but I am sure 2002 may hold the answer.

Little did I know the trek had only begun and the purpose of the meeting was no longer discernible to me.

First Kings 19:1-4 records maybe the greatest pity party by a prophet of God in the history of the Bible:

Ahab told Jezebel all that Elijah had done, and how he had killed all the prophets with the sword. Then Jezebel sent a messenger to Elijah, saying, "So may the gods do to me and more also, if I do not make your life as the life of one of them by this time tomorrow." Then he was afraid, and he arose and ran for his life and came to Beersheba, which belongs to Judah and left his servant there. But he himself went a day's journey into the wilderness and came and sat down under a broom tree. And he asked that he might die, saying, "It is enough; now, O Lord, take away my life, for I am no better than my fathers." (1 Kings 19:1-4, emphasis added)

The wilderness of our lives can drive us to complete despair, even the godliest like Elijah.

When my friend rejected my help, I lost all confidence in my ability to hear from God. I was convinced I should resign from the church I pastor. I was convinced I was a phony. Elijah was trying to make a difference for God. I was trying to make a difference for God. Elijah concluded, "It is enough; now, O Lord, take away my life."

I can't speak for Elijah's pain, but I can describe how I responded to mine.

My naïve obedience like Elijah met the painful disappointment associated with doing what God asks you to do but not seeing the result you were hoping for. This perpetual questioning triggered a pervasive mindset that left me with what I call spiritual PTSD.

As we know from Elijah's life, regardless of how close we walk with God, none of us are immune from this deep depression born out of everyday disappointments. It is hard to see the sorrows that come from the disappointments we have when we naïvely obey God and expect a positive outcome.

Every time I saw 1:23 on license plates, billboards, clocks, price tags, it triggered a pervasive depression that caused me to want to find my own broom tree in the wilderness to die under like Elijah. In these 1:23 a.m. experiences with God, I was learning that *the chaos and confusion caused me to question everything I believed about God and myself.*

Spiritual **PTSD**

Perpetual questioning of a negative situation triggers pervasive anxiety. All of us are searching for something in our present to help us make sense of our past. Wishing something had never happened doesn't solve the puzzle but perpetuates the darkness to become pervasive.

On the world stage in 2002, our nation was at war in Iraq and Afghanistan, searching for the allusive Osama bin Laden. The whole world was looking for him, along with the greatest military in the world, but no evidence could be found of his whereabouts.

Back home in my day-to-day trials of adjusting to the allusive nature of my situation, I would learn eventually that I was settling very quickly into a pervasive depression. I would call this *spiritual PTSD*. In this season I would come home exhausted from the normal work of ministry, plop down in my chair, and listen to the enemy whisper in my ear for hours how much God didn't care about me and how He was making me the laughingstock of the spiritual world.

On the world stage, the difficulty of finding Bin Laden was a global indicator of what the next six years of my life personally would be like regarding the allusive nature of the situation I was dealing with.

I went to a retreat in January of 2002 with a group of leaders. My new friend was one of the participants. I knew that I would see him, and it gave me great angst. Whereas our nation couldn't find its opposition, mine walked right before me. I had to come to terms that I was a victim of his power, and he had swallowed me whole and spit me out, knowing his power gave him the freedom to do as he pleased.

At this retreat, we passed one another in the hallway, he motioned for me to join him at his car as he was leaving. He said to me, "I forgive you for what you did to me." I was speechless. I didn't know what to say, so I said, "Thank you." I walked away, and over time, the rage and anger grew inside of me as I thought about the continued humiliation he put me through and the injustice that I felt toward him because of his marginalization of me and my life.

One interesting thing that came out of that retreat is one of the pastors felt compelled to pray a prophetic prayer. In his prayer he acknowledged some hidden sin that had to do with a sexual nature and that someone present needed to come clean and deal with God before it was too late. After the retreat I walked up to that pastor and asked him why he prayed that. He said he didn't know, it just felt like the Spirit came over him, and words began to fill his mind and mouth. He felt like the Spirit of God loosed his tongue and spoke those words through him. He said when he finished he sat there, confused by what and why he just prayed what he did and wondered what it all meant.

Later I shared with that pastor what I had gone through, and he began to support me through this trial. Over the years that pastor has become a very dear pastor friend of mine. I am very grateful for his friendship. His friendship to me was like God throwing me another lifeline while waiting on Him to do whatever He would do with this situation. I just wished He would hurry up.

When we sought out to find Bin Laden, I doubt anyone in the world, besides Bin Laden maybe, thought it would take us a decade to find him. I too could have never imagined when I sat in the car on 10/23/2001 that this search for resolution and resolve would span well into the decade of my 30s and still have a lasting impact on my life well into my 40s. Some things you just don't see coming in your life. We are all eager to dream when we are younger. We are all ambitious in our own way to grab life by the horns and give the ol' bull a swing. Little do we know that when we grab a hold of the horns of life, it lifts us off the ground and takes us on a journey we could have never imagined. Often times the pain is greater than we could have envisioned, and the payoff seems to be small compared to the price we have paid emotionally with our lives.

I have never been physically or sexually abused and then left to deal with it on my own, but I have lived in a world where I was marginalized and minimized by someone. I remember not long after I had gone through the terrible ordeal, I met with a young couple in our church that was soon to get married, and they were considering making our church their home church. We sat down in my office to talk, and I figured we would discuss theology, church polity, worship style, preaching style, what my favorite color was, and briefly touch on a dozen or so normal categories that people like to discuss before choosing their home church.

We sat down, and the couple immediately asked me about *this* situation. I had no idea how they knew about it, but they began to question me and told me they were informed by a pastor who had spoken with someone that they should be wary of me and avoid me if at all possible. As I sat there and listened to those words, the knives of this allusive mysterious *23* prophetic experience began to rush over me and take me back to every vile image I had seen in my awake hours the past year leading to the painful confrontation. It was painfully obvious to me that he was not going to relent, and this situation was not going anywhere any time soon.

The enemy attacked me often in this season of confusion. I resisted. I fought those voices and those feelings, but like anyone who has been abused, you know that at some point the enemy begins to break you down. The psychological paralysis that you begin to feel from the enemy's never-ending barrage of insults and put-downs eventually leads to the destruction of the will. Early on I was unsure how much I could take of this.

I found myself waking up in the night, saying to myself, *It is not supposed to be like this.* I remember going to bed, saying to myself, *How long, oh Lord?* At night, I would be tormented by visions of "the man" in my sleep.

I would have very vivid dreams of how I was trying to help him, but every time it backfired, and I was left either literally dead in the dreams or at least battered emotionally by the litany of accusations he would level at me.

I found myself consumed by this situation. I would do ministry, spend time with my family, attempt to enjoy sports, go to dinner with someone, attend a gathering of some sort, but somehow, someway, it always led back to this situation. I cannot tell you how many times someone would come up to me in this season of allusive years of intense spiritual warfare and talk to me about how amazing this person was and how important their ministry was to the city.

Not long after this he was voted to become a leader in a prominent Christian organization. While my influence shrank, stalled, and just flat out evaporated before my eyes, his influence continued to grow. I watched him climb the Christian corporate ladder of who's who in America. It made me sick. I weakened in my prayers and in my willingness to trust the Lord; I waivered often. Not only was I watching this play out before my eyes, hearing the barrage of insults in my head belittling me daily, but I also didn't know how to lay to rest the pain I had experienced in the tragic loss of my mother being killed by a drunk driver. I didn't know if God wants us to cry "uncle," but I found myself screaming "UNCLE, relief already!"

Why would God allow me to be humiliated as such and allow him to keep climbing the corporate ladder of who's who for Jesus in America? Why was I marginalized and left to wander and wonder while he sailed to the top of the "I'm the most important Christians" poll in the world? I wasn't in middle school, but it sure did feel like it.

I lived with the ever-present fear of being wrong and being wiped off the map by him. I wondered in this season if God was cruel. I often reflect on what our nation went through during 9/11; just as Osama was trying to destroy our nation, this man was trying to destroy me.

Recently my family was traveling across the United States. We noticed road signs for the Flight 93 Memorial near Shanksville, Pennsylvania. I felt a tug in my heart, even though we were on a schedule to get to a speaking engagement. We took the half hour or so detour and got off the interstate.

We drove through the country, up and down hills, and came to a location seemingly in the middle of nowhere. We took the long, windy drive into the memorial. I expected a couple of signs and a few remarks—boy I was wrong. As we neared the location, I felt the sacredness of this space. I wondered, *Is this because it is bringing back memories of that day?* I asked my kids, some of whom weren't even born in 2001, "Do you feel the heaviness?" They said, "Yes."

There were scores of people there, and we took the walk down the path that directed our eyes to a twenty-thousand-pound boulder that marked the fifty-foot hole the airplane had made when it went down. We walked into the memorial—back and forth through the walls of memorabilia from that day, news clippings, articles found at the crash scene, newscasters recounting the events of the day, presidents of the United States addressing this heroic day. And then there were these phones—when we picked up the receiver, we could listen to Flight 93 passengers leaving answering machine messages for their loved ones because they could not get them on the phone. It was bone chilling. We didn't have to try to cry or conjure emotion. It flowed. We felt it. Their story was our story. It's *our* story. It is the story of courage in the face of evil.

One of the individuals who made a call was passenger Lauren Catuzzi Grandcolas. She was flying home from her grandmother's funeral. She made eight calls to her husband from row 23, seats DEF, but she never got him on the phone. She left this message: "There has been a little problem with the plane, but I am fine and comfortable—for now."

They knew they were going to die and that it probably wouldn't end well, and yet, they knew they had to do something to try and save others.

We know we are going to die—someday.

Their story is our story.

Is that not the story of Jesus? Is that not our story? A story of redemption amidst great sacrifice, sorrow, and imminent death. That's why I pressed into my new friend. I wanted to help him.

Tears filled my eyes as I listened to the sobering messages of these people leaving their final words for their loved ones. One of them reminded me of my mom and the tone of her voice and her final call to me before she died: "Know that I love you . . ." Those words are so powerful but even more so when those are the last words you ever hear from them in this life.

It takes courage to sacrifice your life, but it takes more courage to live when you know you are going to die. One of the great leaders on that plane that day was Todd Beamer who went to Wheaton College. He was presently in a Bible study with some men, studying Dr. Howard Hendricks's book, *A Life of Integrity*. He led the passengers and phone dispatcher in praying Psalm 23. The favor of the Lord was with him. He led the fight with his famous words "let's roll" to take Flight 93 to the ground before the terrorists could fulfill their plan and crash the plane into either the White House or Congress in Washington D.C. These words, "let's roll," became the battle cry of our leadership and nation. Their heroism saved, no doubt, tens of thousands of people, because on any given day, there were upwards of twenty-to-thirty thousand people in Congress.

A guide at the grounds that lives near the memorial said that nine people saw the plane go down. The plane was moving at a speed of 563 miles per hour. One eyewitness said the plane was inverted and flying upside down before it crashed. The passengers were fighting the terrorists and forcing it to the ground. The eyewitness said the plane was so close to the ground he could see the grass reflecting in the metal of the plane. When the plane hit the ground, it disintegrated immediately, killing all forty of the passengers and the four terrorists. It took weeks to comb through the debris and try to piece the sorrow of this event together.

In the midst of the wreckage, a miracle occurred; they found the credit card the terrorists used to put all this together. It was fully intact, and it provided the necessary link for the United States to connect the dots. In the midst of this horrific moment of heroism, I believe God smiled at our nation, these people, and our future.

As my friend Jimmy sometimes says, "All people need is a little hope."[4] And I believe God gave us that little hope on that day as a nation. In the midst of the darkest moments and hours of our lives, He gives us small reminders He is there. He sees. He hears our cries, and He comes to our side.

It doesn't erase the sorrow or bring back the people we love, but it does give us a glimmer of hope in the darkest part of the night. But you still have to walk through this valley of sorrow and suffering.

I often think about all the people who lost loved ones on that day. One of the displays at the memorial was titled "Loss of Life," and it said this:

> *The death toll from the planes' impact and the collapse of the Towers is staggering. Flight 11 hits floors 93–99 of the World Trade Center's North Tower, killing all on board and 1,470 people in and around the building. Flight 175 crashes into floors 77–85 of the South Tower, killing everyone on board and 695 people in and around the building. Additionally, 441 first responders are killed at the World Trade Center site. As Flight 77 hits the west façade of the Pentagon (where 23,000 civilians and military work [another display tells us this]), the impact kills all on board and 125 people in the building. It is not known how many people lose their lives after September 11 as a result of exposure to toxins at Ground Zero.*
>
> *In addition to these deaths, 40 passengers lost their lives on Flight 93 that day.*

The horrific statistics of death make it seemingly impossible to go on, but I know our nation tried to go on. For those who lost loved ones, I know from my own personal experience, you can't replace someone you love—you can only remember, miss them, and as a believer, look forward to the reunion day in heaven.

I wondered, *What do the people of 9/11 feel like who lost loved ones? And here we are, as a nation in war, and we can't find the main person who was responsible for this? How did that feel? How do people go on when their*

---

4.   Jimmy Mellado is president of Compassion International and has shared this message worldwide with those who partner to support the ministry.

loved ones turn up missing, and they have no idea if they are alive or dead?
The cruelty of life is real, and it is ever present in all of our lives,
regardless of our stories. Yes, some atrocities are more obvious than
others, but how many millions, maybe billions, of people live with
the ever-present torture of the loss of a loved one, dignity, hope, the
ability to provide? The list goes on and on.

Our nation so desperately wanted to find Bin Laden, but for
a decade there was no movement, no hope, no insight, no chance.
During those ten years, our nation went on, but I am sure those who
lost their loved ones woke up each morning, wondering, *Does God
care? Does He care about the injustices of this life?* I think about all the
single moms who would now raise their sons without their fathers
present because of their bravery and unfortunate circumstances that
landed them in those Twin Towers on 9/11.

The tragedies of life unfortunately are not a respecter of
persons. The sorrows create a silent but very loud shame that all of
us carry inside ourselves because of circumstances in our lives that
we don't understand and can't explain. We can't help but wonder like
Job, *God, do You see?*

For ten years our nation looked for Bin Laden. For ten years
God knew where he was. For ten years it seems God did nothing.

For six years God knew about my new friend and what he
had done, and in the midst of it, God allowed him to prosper and
continue to experience the fruit of God's favor. For six years God
did not respond to my requests. For six years He let me wander and
wonder. He let me dwell on the mystery of *23* and live in the tension
of not being able to discern His voice. For six years I would set it on
the shelf and say, "God, this is Your life. Do as You wish," only to
take it back again and again and again.

At one point in this journey, Tosha and I had gone away for
a weekend. I was trying to relax. I was trying to let go, but I just
couldn't let go of the angst. It had a firm grasp around my heart and
mind, and it consumed me. Everything I did or read was flavored by
this 1:23 a.m. experience. Finally, Tosha said to me (and rightfully
so), "You have to stop talking to me about this. I can't take hearing
about this all the time."

Scores of times those that were closest to me would tell me, "Maybe he is doing good now and God accomplished what He wanted to accomplish through you, and you just need to move on." Easier said than done. All the time I wondered—I felt in my spirit— I'm sure like our military as they searched for Bin Laden, *He's out there, and we will find him.* It was my burden to bear. It was my ring to carry.

During this season, *The Lord of the Rings* came out, and the wise words of Gandalf the Great brought great comfort to my heart during this season. Frodo said to Gandalf, "I wish this ring would have never come to me." Gandalf responds, "So do all who live to see such times, but that is not for them to decide. You must simply decide what to do with the time you've got."

All of us are searching for something in life in order to make sense of the past situations and relationships of our lives. It is in the midst of these times that we develop spiritual PTSD. This is when I learned that sometimes *obedience to God's voice feels wrong when the results seem negative.*

Spiritual PTSD will trigger at least three things in you: (1) You question if God cares; (2) You doubt your ability to hear God's voice in your everyday life; (3) You start convincing yourself your faith can't survive the darkness. You do the enemy's work for him in your own life. We sink into our lowest moments in life at this time.

If we stop here and wish it never happened, the enemy wins.

Whether it is a nation chasing a global mass murderer, or people trying to put their lives back together after losing a loved one on 9/11, or me chasing an understanding of a divine experience, or you trying to make sense of your sorrows and circumstances, one thing is for sure: wishing something had never happened will not help solve the puzzle. In the darkness, we must keep searching, probing, praying, crying, reaching, hoping, and then when we least expect it, in our future, a breakthrough will come.

Just a little hope!

If we keep going, we learn to find God in our everyday lives, regardless of the outcome. That gives me hope, and I bet it does you too. We eventually learn, God is faithful in the everyday workings of our lives if we don't give up.

Let us be reminded of Todd's example in leading Flight 93 to the ground: "The Lord is our Shepherd, we shall not want" (Psalm 23). Todd and the others went through the valleys, and like them, if we don't give up, we will "dwell in the house of the Lord" (Psalm 27:4) forevermore, one day.

What are you waiting for?

"Let's roll!"

Section 2:
Lost in the Middle

2:31 A.M.

It began again at 2:31 a.m.

The visions that once woke me up at 1:23 a.m. gave way to 2:31 a.m.

There's that devilish *23* haunting me again!

Often I have asked God, "Why do I hear Your voice best at night?" I feel like the response is, "Because that is when you are most vulnerable and willing to listen."

March 18, 2003

Today is the day I seek the Lord and prepare a message. Last night our president announced to us that we are going to war soon with Iraq to take out Saddam Hussein. This is a very scary time in our country. I pray, God, that You are leading our president. Give him humility and wisdom. Help him to lead as we go to war. I pray You protect civilians in the area. May You protect and be sovereign over our military. God, I pray Your will be done, whatever that may be. May You make Yourself known to our people during this time.

I went from the world stage happenings to my little world stage happenings in my journal entry that day.

Last night Tosha was gone to a meeting, so the girls, Joshua, and I stayed home and played together. We had a great time. We turned on some music, and we all four danced together. We had a great time. It was fun watching Christianna shake her little fanny. She is so funny. Anastasha is really learning a lot at her dance class. It was fun to see our little girl growing up and developing skills. I held Joshua last night and danced with him. He had a great time, laughing and kicking his feet. His top front teeth are poking through the gums. He is cute with teeth.

Then in my journal it went from my little world stage happenings back to the world stage happenings. The two worlds collided . . .

Anastasha and I were talking last night about the war. I asked her how she would feel if I got killed in the war. She said, "Sad, but there would be more room in the bed." Meaning, she would get to sleep with mommy. She's funny! She is my calculated cold-hearted child. She is just like me.

Then my journal entry went from world stage and my little world stage colliding to writing about what was going on in the heavenlies when I laid my head down at night to sleep.

A couple of nights ago (Monday morning, 2:31 a.m.) I woke up and went to use the bathroom.

I learned a long time ago that when you wake up in the night there are really only two plausible reasons—for me, at least. It is either God or gas. So I take care of the one I can do something about and usually go back to bed. It quickly becomes very apparent to me in these moments as to whether it was God or gas or both that woke me up. I hear the voice of God best at night when I have been sleeping. Why? I don't know, but that is the way it is. I have asked the Lord numerous times, "Why, Lord, at night?" And the response I get in my head is, "Because that is when you are most still, vulnerable, and willing to listen. That is when I can say the most to you, and you are willing to hear it very clearly."

While I was there I felt the Lord speaking to me. I believe the Lord spoke to me about the situation with "the man." I have been asking when it would come to the surface, and I believe the Lord has been saying "soon" for the past fourteen months.

Early Monday morning I believe he said, "Now." I don't know what "now" means, but it is obviously sooner than "soon." I went back to bed with a sense that God had spoken to me. I wasn't sure though, as I never am, though this time I have less doubt than in the past, less uncertainty. Less need to prove it was Him. I went back to bed, wrestling with this issue, and I believe God spoke very clearly. I believe God gave me Ecclesiastes 7:8: "Finishing is better than starting. Patience is better than pride." I kept reading on to verse nine, "Don't be quick tempered, for anger is the friend of fools."

I want to finish well in this situation. And finishing well means I focus on being patient instead of letting my pride overtake me and cause me to be hasty. Because when my pride takes over then my temper kicks in and I want to fight, literally. Lord, I do not want to be a friend of fools.

I want to be a wise man that waits on You, Lord. I want to find my confidence in Your provision and protection, Lord. I want to find my confidence in Your Sovereign hand, Lord. Teach me, Lord, to trust in You.

On April 5, 2003, I recorded in my journal that our military was inside of Baghdad. The fighting was escalating on the ground just as it was in the heavenlies with my situation.

However, there was one big difference: our nation's troops were literally advancing, and my elders told me to "cool it." I asked them if I could dig for dirt to clear my name in the situation, and they told me to wait and do nothing. I found my earlier journal entry about waiting a whole lot easier to write than to live. However, I am extremely grateful for my elder board, because without them, I would probably not have been able to maintain the level of self-control that I was able to, due to their authority in my life.

Soon after this, my new friend was appointed to be the president of an organization that represented forty-two million Christians. I was stunned by this turn of events. I know this wasn't true, but it felt like it was me against forty-two million Christians who now supported him. My "waiting" was producing odds greater than my heart could take.

Locally, he started holding meetings about me to tell others his version of what I had done to him. I couldn't sleep at night, and it got worse! I felt like the Lord spoke Isaiah 48:7 to me: "They are created now, not long ago; before today you have never heard of them, lest you should say, 'Behold, I knew them.'" I read it and couldn't make any sense of it, and I still can't to this day. But I felt a peace, and I felt like He was trying to convey something to me. Even though I couldn't interpret or understand what He was saying to me, I still felt the peace from being obedient; even though I didn't know how to apply the Word, I felt His presence, and really, that was all I needed. I tell this so everyone can see that when you try to follow God and listen to His voice and respond to His promptings, sometimes it will make no sense to you and may seemingly make no difference; but nonetheless, obedience is obedience.

God doesn't reward your ability to get it right when He speaks to you. He rewards your faithfulness to obey and attempt to do what you think He said to you. But naïve obedience can only carry you so far in your faith journey with Jesus. Eventually, real life beats the optimism out of your faith. And yes, sometimes you will get it wrong. You will not bat a one thousand when it comes to hearing from God, but don't let that keep you from listening and trying to do what you believe He is instructing you to do. I have learned through this experience that *God rewards flawed faithfulness.* And it is your flawed faithfulness that will keep you sane in the midst of the jumbled experiences of your life.

In this season of intense confusion and pain, the visions increased, the dreams increased, and so did the fear. I found it hard to make sense of what was taking place, and I often misunderstood or misinterpreted God's voice in this season. Strangely enough, it was during this season that I and my new friend were invited to Focus on the Family to be one of the first thirty people to see the movie *The Passion of The Christ.* I also met Mel Gibson on that day. Strange happenings all around as I was trying to discern God's directive and will for my life and the things He was revealing to me.

I found myself in this season so desperate that I began to wake up at night, already praying, begging God to take this incredible burden away from me or to expose it, because my heart couldn't take much more of this. It was during this time that God showed mercy to me through Psalm 23. I found myself praying Psalm 23 often. Coincidentally during this time, my good friend Bob unknowingly prayed Psalm 23 over me. It gave me chills. "Yea, though I walk through the valley of the shadow of death, I will fear no evil" (Psalm 23:4 KJV). I needed that prayer. I needed that "coincidence." I needed the grace of God applied to my life through the prayer of a dear friend who cared but didn't know the details of how God had already been ministering to me. He took my burden unknowingly through his prayer and cared for me. Thank you, Bob!

I found my nights in this season full of heart cries, like, *How long, Lord?* I felt like every time, He said, "The end is near." My response back to Him would be, *I don't know how much longer I can take this.*

July 5, 2003

I found my heart lonely, agitated, and critical. Tosha and I argued Monday night and didn't connect very well. We went to sleep in silence. My heart got worse Tuesday. I felt myself fighting in my prayers the spirits of hell. I don't even think I can describe in words what I was feeling except torment. I quoted Psalm 23 in my sleep Tuesday night. It is a fight I have never experienced. I said to the Lord, "I feel protected yet exposed. I feel peaceful yet angry." I have never battled the demons of another's life or mine like I have in this situation. I have no idea why God chose me to bear this, but I accept it. I consider it an honor to bear up under burdens, for He has seen fit to count me trustworthy in His kingdom. I must confess, "I so long for this to end." I know Tosha does.

Wednesday was worse. By the end of the day, I felt possessed and tormented by agitating thoughts, accusations mostly directed toward those I love the most. I stayed in silence and fought the tormenting thoughts—the greatest enemy you can't see; the greatest fights you will never know the scope of. The significance of the battle will not always be seen at the time of the battle, but we must fight. For the darkness will not last forever, and when the light comes, we will feel and see the significance of our battle. "Yea, though, I walk through the valley of the shadow of death, I will fear no evil: for thou art *with* me" (Psalm 23:4 KJV). I believed I was in that valley at that time. Tosha told me, "You look evil." I responded that I felt the evil around me.

During this time, someone in our church sent me a word they felt they had received from God, and it moved me. It said, "The Spirit of Moses is coming soon." I await deliverance. This "prompting of the Holy Spirit"—or "prophetic" message, if you like—made me feel like I was in bondage like the children of Israel were in Moses' day in Egypt. I took this to mean that God was sending the Spirit of Moses to deliver me. It gave me the strength to hang on.

Wednesday night I thought I was losing my mind. I have never felt some of the things I felt that night. I thought I was going insane. I wasn't afraid of dying—I welcomed it. I don't know how to describe what I went through. I hated it, but I couldn't stop it. I felt like, and feel now, God used it to purify me and break me more. We went to bed early that night, and when I woke up Thursday morning, it was gone.

Thursday was a perfect day. Our family had a fun day, and the demons slept. The Lord gave us a gift!

During this season, God gave me Deuteronomy 6:10-15:

And when the Lord your God brings you into the land . . . to give you—with great and good cities that you did not build, and houses full of all good things that you did not fill, and cisterns that you did not dig, and vineyards and olive trees that you did not plant—and when you eat and are full, then take care lest you forget the Lord, who brought you out of the land. It is the Lord your God you shall fear. You shall not go after other gods, for the Lord your God in your midst is a jealous God—lest the anger of the Lord your God be kindled against you, and he destroy you from off the face of the earth.

I learned that night when I thought the enemy was going to literally crush me, that God had me and that the promise of Deuteronomy 6:10-15 was not just for Israel but for me as well— and more importantly, for you too. *Thank You, Lord, for Your provision. When we are weak . . . Lord, You are strong and mighty to save!* He can, and He does *bless us through our flawed faithfulness when our naïve obedience has drowned.*

Claim His promise of Deuteronomy 6:10-15—the Lord, through your flawed faithfulness, is bringing you into the good land of your life.

231 JUMBLED EXPERIENCES

I t shouldn't be this way."

I said this to myself at least two million times during this difficult prophetic season of my life.

I watched my new friend from a distance ignore the promptings of the Lord. I watched his success soar and my confidence in hearing from Him plummet.

During this very low season of my life, we got a call at our church office for me to go visit a woman's mother who was in a special care facility just down the street from our church. The woman had recently come to Christ through our church and was concerned about her mother because she was in the prime of her life but dying of a brain tumor. Honestly, not knowing the woman or her mother, I reluctantly said yes to going and visiting her. What would I say to a total stranger?

We scheduled the appointment, and the young woman agreed to meet me there and pray with her mother. I showed up. She never did. To this day I don't know why she didn't show up. I was sitting in the waiting room of this care facility, waiting for this young woman

I had never met to arrive so we could pray with her mother who was dying—a woman with whom I had never met. Did I mention to you that I'm an introvert? This was the only time I had ever been with a total stranger who was dying. I was freaked out, but it got worse! It always does.

The nurse came out to the waiting room and said, "She is ready to see you now." I looked around and there was no young woman there to accompany me to her mother's bedside to pray and prepare her to die.

Honestly, if the nurse had not been standing there, I would have bolted as fast as I could. Everything inside of me screamed, *RUN, FOREST, RUN!*

I politely rose from my chair and joined her down the long hallway toward this woman's room. The nurse saw me into her room. She was the only patient in the room. The nurse had pulled a chair up beside her bed and said, "You sit here." I sat down, and the nurse left the room. I don't know why, but she closed the door as well.

Here I was, seated at the bedside of a total stranger who was getting ready to die. She was fully sedated and unconscious because of the excruciating pain she was going through physically. In the background there was Christian music playing.

This woman was maybe in her late 40s to early 50s. I sat there just a few feet away from her and observed her lifeless body in that bed, knowing she would never get out of that bed in this lifetime. I kept hearing in my head, *It shouldn't be this way. It shouldn't be this way. It shouldn't be this way!*

Her face was sunken in from the dehydration of the chemotherapy she had taken. She had a doo-rag on her head to cover where the chemo had taken her glory. She was a shell of who I presumed she had once been in her life. Honestly it was more than I could bear. I was already going through a very difficult season in my own life, and now here I was, sitting beside a total stranger who was soon to die.

What happened next surprised me. I opened my mouth, and I started to talk to her. I started to weep. I wept uncontrollably for some time. I never got to say goodbye to my mom. She called me and told me she loved me, and I the same to her, and the next time I saw her, she was in a casket, dead.

I sat by this total stranger's bed, took her hand, and wept like a baby. I talked to her about her life like I was talking to my own mom. I often glanced over my shoulder during this time to make sure there wasn't anyone else in the room. I felt crazy but free.

I commenced to pray over her. I asked the Lord for grace and mercy over her life. I asked the Lord to receive her into His hands. I asked the Lord to heal her in this life or the next but to allow her suffering to end in this life. I prayed and prayed and prayed. It was so freeing and such a powerful moment for me personally. I ended my prayer and leaned over to her ear and whispered, "See you in heaven."

I got up and opened the door and walked out of her room.

As I walked out of her room, I turned and noticed the number of her room was 231. The number caught my attention because God had been waking me up at 2:30 and then at 2:31 a.m.

I wondered often of what the significance was of this number as I lay awake during the wee hours of the mornings I couldn't sleep. I had assumed that Psalm 23:1 was the scope of it: "The Lord is my shepherd, I shall not want."

As I walked out of that room, I said to myself, *It shouldn't be this way. Lord, why is it this way?* When I turned and saw the room number—231—I felt like the Lord said, "Look at the number, 231. The numbers are jumbled; they are not in a correct order like 123. They are twisted and maimed by life. Everyone has 231 experiences in their life and must learn to make the best of them, because even though they shouldn't be that way, they are, and they may never know why in this life."

I had no idea that God would use a total stranger in my life to teach me this lesson. My mom is one of my 231 experiences. As I write this, she has been gone now for almost 23 years in just a few months. Never in a million years did I dream God would orchestrate such an event in my life during such a hard time in my life to teach me the value of 231 experiences. We all have them. We all struggle to understand them. The psalmist said it best in Psalm 23:1, "The Lord is my Shepherd, I shall *not* want. He makes me to lie down in green pastures. He leads me beside still waters" (emphasis added).

I have battled for almost 23 years to make sense of my mom's tragic death at the hands of a drunk driver. I have fought hard to find meaning and reason to this seemingly senseless act of destruction and death. And in 2003, God seated me next to a total stranger and taught me a very important lesson: *We all have 231 experiences we carry.* He sees them. He knows them. He is intimately acquainted with them. No, He doesn't always heal them, change them, solve them, or even seemingly make them better in this life. He does allow us to live in the tension of the 231 experiences of our lives. He allows us to struggle. No, I don't like this, and I am sure you don't either.

Lest you think "bad" things only happen to the kids God doesn't like, during this season of my life, Job 23 became a very important chapter to me. Job was asking the question I was asking when my mom died, when "the man" was getting away with "murder," and when I was sitting beside that total stranger's bed: *Where is* God *in all of this?*

Job says in Job 23:1-17,

Then Job answered and said: "Today also my complaint is bitter; my hand is heavy on account of my groaning. Oh, that I knew where I might find him, that I might come even to his seat! I would lay my case before him and fill my mouth with arguments. I would know what he would answer me and understand what he would say to me. Would he contend with me in the greatness of his power? No; he would pay attention to me. There an upright man could argue with him, and I would be acquitted forever by my judge. Behold, I go forward, but here is not there, and backward, but I do not perceive him; on the left hand when he is working, I do not behold him; he turns to the right hand, but I do not see him. But he knows the way that I take; when he has tried me, I shall come out as gold. My foot has held fast to his steps; I have kept his way and have not turned aside. I have not departed from the commandment of his lips; I have treasured the words of his mouth more than my portion of food. But he

is unchangeable, and who can turn him back? What he desires,
that he does. For he will complete what he appoints for me, and
many such things are in his mind. Therefore I am terrified at
his presence; when I consider, I am in dread of him. God has
made my heart faint; the Almighty has terrified me; yet I am
not silenced because of the darkness, nor because thick darkness
covers my face. (emphasis added)

Can you relate? Job continues on for almost another twenty chapters. He understands your 231 experiences. He had a few in his own life as well, and if there is anyone outside of Jesus that didn't deserve to suffer, Job would be on the top of the list.

How are you handling your 231 experiences right now in your life? What are you doing with them? The day before I wrote this chapter, I had two different people tell me of three Christians who decided they no longer believed God existed and that they had become atheists. Certainly that is an option. Certainly all of us can stare our 231 experiences in the face long enough that we convince our minds that God no longer exists, but our hearts know differently. Our hearts know 231 experiences are real, and there is *no* hope of being "unwanton" without a shepherd to *lead* us beside the still waters in the midst of these times.

Sitting beside her bed, I found the "still" waters. Thanks to the medication, she was stable and at peace in the midst of excessive pain, and I got to see an example of the kind of "medication" God can be in our lives spiritually, in spite of our 231 experiences. I learned that day that *regardless of the jumbled situations in our lives, flawed faithfulness is still a choice we can all make.*

In the midst of this very painful 231 season of our lives, we learned that we were pregnant with our fourth child, who we would later learn was Annalarie McKenzie Faith. Her name means "crowned with honor and faith." We have learned over and over again, it is impossible to live the 231 experiences without a crown of honor and faith. It is what *protects* us from ourselves, because see, only *you* can keep yourself from believing. No matter how bad the 231 experiences are, if you say to yourself, *No matter the cost, I believe,* you will be amazed at the experiences that you will have that lie just beyond the bend of this 231 season of your life.

Say this with me right now . . .

This 231 experience shouldn't be this way, but God has given me a different 231, Psalm 23:1 (through verse 4), to combat these thoughts: "The Lord is my Shepherd, I shall not want, He makes me lie down in green pastures. He leads me beside still waters. Yeah, though I walk through the valley of the shadow of death, I will fear no evil [231 experience] for you are with me Lord."

THE BIG FISH STORY

11

S o many people are paralyzed by their fear that they will get God's will wrong in their life—that they will mess it up. Because of this, they choose to do nothing at all.

My dad used to say when I was child, "Let's do something, even if it is wrong." He was joking (*I think!*). But the truth is, anything we do in our lives we will do wrong to some degree. None of us will have one day of perfection in this life.

I often say to my first-born perfectionist daughter, "Anastasha, you know you will never have one day of perfection in this life?"

She responds, "I know, and it drives me crazy just thinking about it."

Everyone knows the story of Jonah and the big fish. The Lord asked Jonah to go to Nineveh, his arch-enemies, the ones that had caused him and his people the *most* pain in their lives. God asked Jonah to go and preach repentance to them, and if they repented, God would spare their city.

Jonah thought about it for a bit and said, "No thanks, God! I have a different plan." And he turned and headed the opposite direction to Joppa. You can't blame Jonah. What God asked Jonah to do would be the equivalent of God asking a Christian to go to the Taliban or Al-Qaeda, or the latest terrorists, like ISIS, and say to them, "Repent or God will destroy you." We all pretty much know how that would go today. So you can't blame Jonah for saying, "Thanks, but no thanks, God!"

However, this is what God asked Jonah to do. Because he didn't do it, Jonah 1:17 records, "And the Lord appointed a great fish to swallow up Jonah. And Jonah was in the belly of the fish three days and three nights."

Some people believe this is an allegory and never happened. I'm not one of those people, and neither is *Jesus for that matter.* There is no minor prophet Jesus spoke of more in the Gospels than Jonah. Jesus said in Matthew 12:40, "For just as Jonah was three days and three nights in the belly of the great fish, so will the Son of Man be three days and three nights in the heart of the earth."   I could belabor the point with Jesus, but I won't, because if you care to know more, you can do a search and read the different times Jesus mentions the story of Jonah in the New Testament. It is almost as if Jesus knew many would think of Jonah as just a "big fish" story and not a true story.

I remember my childhood days with my dad as my pastor. My dad was really good at memorizing things, especially if they had a bit of humor attached to them. One of my favorite poems my dad memorized was the story of Jonah. It goes something like this . . .

Now listen my friends, and I'll tell you a tale,
How old Jonah the prophet got caught by the whale.
The whale caught poor Jonah and, bless your dear soul,
He not only caught him, but swallowed him whole.
A part of this story is awfully sad,
It is how a big city went to the bad,
When the Lord saw those people with such wicked ways,
He said, "I can't stand them more'n forty more days!"

He spoke to old Jonah and said, "Go and cry
To those hard hearted people and tell them that I
Give them forty days more to get humbled down,
And if they don't do it, I'll tear up their town."
Jonah heard the Lord speaking and he said, "No,
That's against my religion, and I won't go.

Those Nineveh people mean nothing to me,
And I'm against foreign missions, you see."

He went down to Joppa and there, in great haste,
He boarded a ship for a different place;
The Lord looked down on that ship and said He,
"Old Jonah is fixing to run off from me."
He set the wind blowing with squeaks and with squeals,
And the sea got rowdy and kicked up its heels;
Old Jonah confessed it was all for his sin;
The crew threw him out, and the whale took him in.

The whale said, "Old fellow, don't you forget,
I am sent here to take you in out of the wet,
You will get punished aright for your sin."
So he opened his mouth, and poor Jonah went in.
On beds of green seaweed that fish tried to rest,
He said, "I will sleep while my food I digest."
But he got mighty restless and sorely afraid,
And he rumbled inside as the old prophet prayed.

The third day that fish rose up from his bed
With his stomach tore up and a pain in his head;
He said, "I must get to the air mighty quick,
For this wicked backslider is making me sick."
He winked his big eyes and wiggled his tail
And pulled for the shore to deliver his mail;
He stopped near the shore and looked all around,
And spewed old Jonah right up on the ground.

Poor Jonah thanked God for His mercy and grace,
And turning around to the whale made a face.
He said, "After three days I guess you have found
A good man, old fellow, is hard to keep down."
He stretched himself out with a yawn and a sigh
And sat down in the sun for his clothing to dry;
He thought how much better his preaching would be,
Since from Whale Seminary he had a degree.

When he had rested and dried in the sun,
He started for Nineveh, right on the run;
He thanked his dear Father in heaven above
For His tender mercy and wonderful love.
And thought he was nearly three days late,
He preached from the time he entered the gate,
Till the whole population repented and prayed.
And by God's great mercy, His vengeance was stayed.

Now friends, when you disobey, remember this tale,
When you run from God's call, look out for the whale;
Wherever God calls you is the place you should go,
And He will go with you His Word tells you so.

(Author Unknown)[5]

That line, "When you run from God's call, look out for the whale," stands out to me in my story. Around the two-year anniversary of the big confrontation with "the man," we went to the doctor for an ultrasound of our fourth child, Annalarie.

During the ultrasound the technician identified the baby for us and said, "Look, the baby has her hands crossed. Looks like the baby is praying." Now my wife, Tosha, probably doesn't like me comparing her to a whale, but I found myself like Jonah, like Annalarie, in the belly of the whale—not because I disobeyed but because I obeyed. I was continually begging God to remove the situation from me. Like Jonah, I wanted to die. I wanted out of this pressure cooker.

A couple of weeks later, on October 23, 2003, I recorded one of the most important entries of my life during this season.

October 23, 2003

Today marks the two-year anniversary of my confrontation with my new friend and his presbytery. If someone would have told me then that two years would pass from that date and nothing would happen, I certainly would not have believed them, but here we are. I have felt like Jonah for two years now.

---

5. Although the source is unknown, the earliest date recorded is 1933 in a field recording by James Howard, "The Old Fish Song" (AFS 74A, 1933).

Jonah 4:3 says, "Just kill me now, Lord!" I'd rather be dead than alive, because nothing I predicted is going to happen.

However, 150 years after Jonah prophesied it, it came true in the book of Nahum. I must, like Jonah, trust in the sovereign hand of God. This situation with "the man" is not over, but it is no longer up to me. It is between him and his God just as Nineveh is no longer Jonah's business. It is between Nineveh and God. Help me, Lord, to continue to relinquish control and trust You.

Last night Tosha and I went to dinner and talked about this very thing. We talked about this never-ending situation with my new friend and what role this plays in our fourth child. I told her when we saw the baby last week on the ultrasound and it had its hands together, praying, it brought tears to my eyes and an instant connection. I later thought about Jonah and how he was in the whale's belly, praying (not that Tosha is a whale!). I got this picture of a praying prophet inside of Tosha's belly. I got a sense that our fourth baby should be named Jonah, though I have no idea if it is a boy because of the position of the baby in the womb during the ultrasound. I believe this baby symbolizes my struggle with God. I have been very angry with God, but I have submitted myself to Him as Jonah did in the whale's belly.

Jonah means dove—*a sent dove from God to bear a message to a people he didn't like and knew God would spare and didn't want God to spare them even if they repented. If I am honest, I have felt the same toward my new friend. I don't want God to spare him— not because I am jealous, but if God spares him in his obstinate sin toward Him, then God's justice or rule doesn't exist. My purpose for taking my directive from God's hand is futile. The same futility Jonah felt. If I do not fulfill God's purpose for my life, I have no purpose. If God's directive to me seems to have no purpose, then what is the point in living, especially living for God?*

If God is not just, then why live for God? Why not just live for myself? Which has been a huge temptation the last two years. But somewhere along the way, I have died to myself in a way that I really can't even describe. I am not the same man I was when this all started over two years ago when God woke me up.

I can't help but feel this whole process was to redeem me from the path I was on and the destruction that awaited me. Personally, I do not believe my new friend is going to turn back from his destructive ways. He did momentarily in that car that day, but as time goes on, his heart gets harder.

Do I wish ill on him? No. If he called me today and said he needed help, I would be there immediately. What I hope is what Jonah hopes. Is that God will be just and carry out who He is, for without that, I have no purpose. Life is futile without God's purpose. I believe God's purpose for me was to confront "the man." I must now wait for Nahum 1:3: "The Lord is slow to get angry, but his power is great, and he never lets the guilty go unpunished" (emphasis added).

I must wait on God's sovereign hand.

Last night Tosha and I talked about naming our fourth child Jonah Benjamin McKenzie Williams, if it is a boy.

I told Tosha last night that strange things keep happening to me in regard to the fish symbol. Last week I was brushing my teeth and looked down and on my shirt was a small piece of string, clinging to my shirt in the shape of a fish. I immediately thought of the rug in the girls' bathroom that has three fish on it. Then I thought of the situation with "the man" that led me to think of the baby that made me think of Jonah. I have no idea what any of this means. Maybe nothing. But Jonah, 3 days, a fish, "the man," and my new baby have some interpolation. I don't know the connection, but I am anxious to know.

If the baby in Tosha's belly is a girl, then I am thoroughly confused again. It is fine with me if it is a girl, but it seems these events point toward a boy. Certainly time will reveal all.

Time told us that little praying baby was a girl. Her name is Annalarie McKenzie Faith, and she is very sensitive to the promptings of the Holy Spirit—I believe she is the most "prophetic" child we have. I was wrong about the details. I share this because it is impossible to bat one thousand when you are trying to discern what God is saying to you. I missed it, but guess what? I'm glad I did. God gave us an amazing little girl who is uniquely gifted prophetically, and her name represents the faith she has.

When you and I are in the midst of the pressure cooker, the belly of the whale, it is easy to assume the details and to assume you know more than you do about the details. When you are in the midst of your 231 experiences, don't sweat the details. As you can tell, I tried to find God in the lint on my clothes. But when I get to heaven, I don't believe God will say to me, "Kelly, your biggest failure is that you tried too hard to see me in the details of your life." I think God can truly be seen everywhere.

You won't be right about all the details, and you will be tortured by the *why* and the *when*. I can't tell you how many times I got the *when* wrong when I was trying to discern what God was doing and when He was going to do it. You will be wrong about a lot of what God tells you in this life, but rest assured, none of the details will keep God from fulfilling His plan. Just like with Jonah, God gets what God wants, *even in spite of you.*

I love this closing thought from Jonah 2:1, 10: "Then Jonah prayed to the Lord his God from the belly of the fish. . . . And the Lord spoke to the fish, and it vomited Jonah out upon the dry land."

Jonah got some of the details wrong, but God obviously still used him. God can and will use you and me.

Don't give up on seeing and finding God in the midst of your "fish belly" experiences. I have learned that *you will be wrong a lot in this life; however, flawed faithfulness can and will be used to fulfill God's perfect plan for your life.*

None of us need one perfect day in our lives to fulfill His perfect plan for our lives. That's pretty cool!

WAITING ON GOD

12

E verybody is waiting for something. I have no idea what it is like
to be in a fish's belly for three days while waiting to be delivered
by the Lord.

I do know, however, what it is like to wait for years for God to
vindicate me in the situation with "the man."

I don't know what you are waiting for, but I have a sneaky
suspicion you do.

During this lengthy season of waiting on God to do something,
to show Himself faithful, to reveal in this situation that His holiness
matters, all I could do was wait.

While waiting, God brought many Scriptures to mind during
my daily devotions. One in particular caught my attention in Isaiah
49:23. "Those who wait for me will never be put to shame."

My question, *Then why is it that waiting brings so much shame
into our lives?* I did what God asked me to do (I thought), and my
life seemingly stalled out while his career and church soared. I'm
embarrassed to admit this, but this question and tension haunted me
during this prolonged season of waiting.

I found myself wearing down from the perpetual burdens of
this situation and growing more and more angry toward God and
depressed in my spirit. I was tired of being discouraged.

What do you do when you are tired of being discouraged?

You ready for this?

You wait.

I have learned this lesson over and over again: *flawed faithfulness requires us, as creatures bound by time, to wait on God when we are discouraged and don't know what to do.*

You intentionally say to yourself, *I will wait on God who, in His time, will not allow me to be put to shame.* This is easier said than done. However, my experiences over the years with God tell me that when I can no longer carry the burdens He has asked me to bear on His behalf, He will send an experience to renew my hope. This reminds me, He is truly doing something in this situation.

Faith and trust are the best health food for your soul. My friend Jimmy sometimes says, "People only need a little hope to keep going."

I agree.

On December 2, 2003, God sent a sliver of hope to my experience to remind me that He was up to something, and that something was occurring behind the scenes.

December 2, 2003

Last week a woman in our church told my sister that she was at my new friend's church, dropping off her kids for an activity with their home school program. The woman had met him once before and talked with him, somehow mentioning she attended the church I pastor. This time he approached her and ask her about me and if I had mentioned the movie Mel Gibson has made regarding the life of Christ. She told him I had mentioned it a couple of times. He was curious as to whether I had mentioned the website. The night after this was told to me I was troubled. I arose from bed about 2:30 a.m. to pray and seek the Lord. I felt confirmation through the Word of God's protection. I wait on God.

God is certainly using this situation in my life to shape me to be the man He wants me to be.

Lord, how long?

A week later, I recorded in my journal . . .

December 9, 2003

I feel happy today. I don't feel extremely burdened. It is a strange feeling. I feel like God has a future for us. I feel like He has been pruning us the last two years, and we are going into a season of growth. The last 24–30 months my heart has been very hard in a lot of ways. The emotional anguish has been very intense. I don't even feel the emotional angst toward my new friend that I did two weeks ago.

I feel a peace I haven't felt in years, literally. The past 2 ½ years have been very difficult emotionally and for our church relationally. But like Paul in Acts 27, we have weathered the storm and we are better for it. Like Paul, we entered the ship a slave, but He is raising us up as the captain. He is pouring out His Spirit on us.

What a difference a prayer and a decision to wait can make!

After this, my new friend's behavior became erratic. His popularity and success continued to soar, but his behavior and what I would call the *spirit of Saul* started to take deeper root in his actions.

In the midst of this, I had a very good mentor and friend, Doug, go to be with the Lord. I miss that man! He was a faithful Navigator for many years before he went to be with the Lord. Doug, along with others, were humanly why I survived this season of my life. Doug and his wife, Priscilla, are what I like to call *good people!*

During the midst of the push/pull tug of waiting, life, all of life, continues to unfold before our eyes. Most of life happens to us, and some of life we choose. This was one of those days where life happened to us.

January 17, 2004

There are some times in life when the struggle is greater than the effort to overcome. It doesn't mean I am a failure. It means I am human. I am limited. My job is to keep a short account on sin. "I am sorry" is in order often. I can't be afraid to say it. It doesn't mean I am a failure, it means I am human. The same is true for the one asking forgiveness of me. Thank You, Lord, for reteaching me such a simple but valuable principle.

Thursday was a hard day for our family and especially Tosha. That night she needed to get away, so she went to dinner and shopping with Ellen (my sister). While she was out, I took care of Joshua and the girls. After dinner I was cleaning up and I noticed a puddle of something on the kitchen floor under Joshua's highchair. Then I noticed it was dripping from his chair. I later learned it was diarrhea. It was bad.

About the same time Christianna threw up. It was amazing. I had two screaming kids, poop on the floor, and throw up! I was gagging, it was so bad! Looking back, it is comical now, but certainly not funny at the time. I was exhausted by the end of the evening. However, it felt good to serve my children and love them in such a way. I want to be more of a servant to them, though I struggle in this area. I am not a hands and feet person. I am used to being out in front, but I am learning what true leadership is and is not. I am growing as a father. I am becoming a good Dad. I am learning how to love my kids into a real relationship with Jesus Christ. Teach me, Lord, how to be a good father.

Why did I just record that journal entry in this book? Because it is easy to fixate on what you are waiting for in life and let the important lessons of life pass you by. Don't forget to look down now and then—the dripping diarrhea and vomit may just be God's plan for your life today.

January 31, 2004

Wednesday I learned my new friend is hosting a secret prayer meeting on Fridays from 10 p.m.–midnight. He shared, with this group, that he is no longer a part of the citywide pastors' network because they hurt his feelings. (I was a part of that network.)

February 3, 2004

The sadness of my new friend continues. It seems like daily I hear of yet another tragedy about his leadership/theology/or ethics. I believe he is coming unraveled at his emotional seams.

February 28, 2004

I woke up feeling strange this morning. I don't really know why, but I have a strange feeling in my gut. Something doesn't feel right. Something feels lost. I came in this morning [to the office] and there was a mass mailout in my box from my new friend. He had a picture of himself praying over Mel Gibson, and then there was a huge picture of him sitting on a bar stool, talking. His success is amazing. He was in the paper last week revealing his plans to build an $18 million facility that will seat 7,500. It will be the largest in the state, both sacred and secular. It is very confusing to me. I am trying to trust God that the outcome of this will be good and not demand the outcome I am looking for from this. I am trying my hardest to stay submitted to the Lord, but at times I find it very difficult to do. I want to fully trust my Lord that He is sovereign, and theologically I believe it, but sometimes I struggle practically. Of late I have wanted to call him, but for what reason? I want to control the situation. I must submit myself to the Lord and His will. Lord, Your ways are certainly not my ways.

March 2, 2004

I begin this day emotionally exhausted. I am tired mentally. My wife and I keep succeeding at miscommunicating. We are both completely spent and emotionally exhausted. Our tanks are empty. Joshua has not felt very well and Tosha has not slept well the last two nights. Tosha is twelve days away from being induced, if we induce on the fifteenth, which I hope we do.

In other news, I saw my new friend on the local evening news Sunday night. He broke ground on his one hundred thousand *square foot, $18 million arena/ auditorium this past Sunday. It is supposed to be done January 2005. He also just got back from the Middle East where he met with the prime minister of Israel. It is all so very confusing to me. Lord, help me this day to commit that situation to You. I am so weary of laboring over that issue. Lord, may Your will be done.*

On March 15, 2004, our fourth child, Annalarie McKenzie Faith, was born. I recorded this in my journal from that experience:

March 15, 2004

The baby was born. She immediately cried. There was a sea of arms, so I couldn't see the sex of the baby. Tosha cried out and said, "Is it a boy?" And the nurse responded, "It is a girl." Boy, did I miss hearing God on that one. I was confused for a few seconds and then elated by the joy of our new little baby girl. She arrived in the world at 6:35 p.m. She is beautiful.

I thought the Lord had revealed to me that this was a boy and his name would signify the end of the saga I have faced with my new friend. But I was wrong. And you know what? I am more than OK with being wrong. I am so glad to have a beautiful girl.

On March 21, 2004, I wondered in my journal entry if Annalarie would be our "prophetic prophetess." She has proven to be the most prophetic child in our family. She senses, discerns, and observes things at a very high level, similar to myself. Is it a coincidence that she has this gift? I think not. Nothing is lost in God's economy, if we . . .

Wait on Him!

SHAME'S STAIN REMAINS

S hame, the stain that remains!
Something doesn't have to be your fault for you to feel shame.

When you and I are vulnerable and the opposite of what we expect happens, that can lead to a deep-seated sense of betrayal and a feeling of complete futility and shame for even attempting to be vulnerable with God or another human being.

Brené Brown is presently known as the leading vulnerability specialist in the United States right now. She has written a number of books, two of which deal with the issue of shame. I am presently reading both of them. The first is *I Thought It Was Just Me (But It Isn't): Making the Journey from "What Will People Think" to "I Am Enough."* The second book is *Daring Greatly*.

Though I don't agree with all of Brené's worldview on certain social and moral issues of the day, I find her writings to have been very freeing and even liberating for me personally.

Her books have helped me discover personally that I have been a victim of the story I am sharing with you. I don't see myself as having done something heroic in this story. I see myself as having done what God asked me to do but feeling like a failure because the outcome in this story is not the one I hoped for or expected.

Brené says in *Daring Greatly*, "Shame thrives on secret keeping." For over a decade now I have kept a "secret." Why? Probably out of respect for my perpetrator, similar to what someone else would feel if they were victimized or abused by someone in their life. I am not saying that what I have experienced even remotely matches practically what others have endured at the hands of their perpetrators, but I do know the spirit behind this sort of ordeal. I have lived long enough to know that even when a person is "discovered," it doesn't remove the stain you feel from the actions and words they used against you in that process.

Being "found out" doesn't take away the stain you feel in your everyday life, and it has a way of changing you and leaving you battered and even potentially ashamed that you gave that much of your energy and thoughts on a *vain* endeavor that seemed to end no better than it started.

All of us are victimized by something. I am not suggesting that we just cry victim and give up, but we have to acknowledge how we have been impacted by the perpetrators of our lives. For me, because of my prophetic experience with God, I sought out my eventual perpetrator. My new friend that I sought to help became my attacker. I don't know who your "perpetrator" is, but like Jesus had in Judas, I am confident we all have at least one in our life, if not more.

How do we deal with the shame that stains that comes from our perpetrators?

Brené says, "You're only as sick as your secrets." She makes a huge point over and over again that you can't fight shame with shame, and that is why it has taken me so long to get to a place where I can write this *in peace* and not *in anger and vindication*. Oh, I am sure we never reach completely pure motives where we write for the sake of redemption, but I do believe I have come to a place where I can write and not seek to shame my perpetrator in this. I contacted my new friend and asked him all these years later for us to work to redeem this together, and he declined. I believe no situation or person is beyond redemption if all parties are willing to participate.

Maybe someday redemption can occur—I keep praying for it, until God redeems things and people we long to see redeemed. How do we deal with the shame we feel from trying to help others?

Brené says in *Daring Greatly*, "Own your story! Don't bury it and let it fester or define you." She often says this aloud: "If you own this story you get to write the ending." When we bury the story, we forever stay the subject of the story. If we own the story, we get to narrate the ending.

As Carl Jung said, "I am not what has happened to me. I am what I choose to become."

As a Christian, I would add, if we own the story, we get to continue to see how God is narrating the ending. We are not just what has happened to us, but we are also who God is making us to be through those difficult and often shaming 231 experiences of our lives.

Romans 8:28 reminds us, "All things work together for the *good* of those who love Him and are called according to His purpose" (emphasis added).

Never give up on this promise as a follower of Jesus Christ.

March 30, 2004

I awoke this morning, interceding for my family. I felt like God was speaking to me, but I could not clearly hear what He was saying. I just know His voice made my heart very excited. I am anxious to see what is ahead in my life.

For whatever reason my new friend has been heavy on my heart again today. I don't know why but I was compelled to get out the letter that "the man's" wife wrote me soon after the confrontation. I reread it and was taken back to those painful moments. It was insightful to read again. I wonder what compelled her to write that letter, and now 2 ½ years later here we are.

My new friend is building a large auditorium in a megachurch. He is president of a national organization, and the list goes on and on. Since the confrontation, the church I pastor has outwardly stayed roughly the same size. I must admit that part is confusing, but I trust God and am convinced I did what my God asked me to do.

Hebrews 11:6 says, "God rewards those who sincerely seek Him."

Lord, You have blessed me in many internal ways, not to mention the two wonderful children You have given me in the last three years. You are kind and gracious, God, and I am very thankful to be counted Your servant. Teach me to be patient and wait on You to reveal Your plan and purpose behind this almost three-year ordeal I have experienced with "the man."

Help me to trust You, Lord. I am so anxious, Lord! It feels like You are doing something, and I am anxious to be a part of it and experience it. Help me to wait on You, Lord. Help me to trust You, Lord.

Waiting gets easier when you trust the one you are waiting on. The opposite of shame is trust.

Why does waiting feel so shameful? Because you don't trust the one you are waiting on. As painful as that is for me to admit, that is what I learned about shame while waiting on the Lord to vindicate the situation with "the man." Trust diminishes shame. Real relationship is what erases the shame of our lives. When we are known by God and others without secrets, and we trust those sources, we walk in minimal to no shame. Shame comes from fear. Trust comes from love. Love and trust are greater than fear and shame. The Bible tells us this in 1 John 4:18-19: "There is no fear in love, but perfect love casts out fear. For fear has to do with punishment, and whoever fears has not been perfected in love. We love because he first loved us."

I did what I believe God asked me to do through a prophetic vision, and it led to me being tortured and tormented by the person I was trying to help. How could I do what God asked me to do and yet my new friend is the one who seemed to have prospered from it? If I chose not to trust the Lord, then fear was my only option, and fear leads to shame. If I chose to trust the Lord, then the result was love. It has taken me a long time, but I am headed down the trust and love path of this ordeal in my life. But rest assured, it has taken me over a decade to get there. Shame and fear are very powerful forces in the universe and close to our daily existence. Trust and love are more powerful forces in the universe but further from our daily existence. They can only be found in the God who made you.

In this battle I have learned that *flawed faithfulness resists the shame of perceived defeat and replaces it with trust in the Author of our lives.*

We must say these important words to God: "I don't understand, but I trust You."

This trust I was learning did not end the battle, but it gave me the little hope I needed to replace the defeat I felt with trust and continue on.

In the midst of this shame versus trust battle I was having with God, my new friend and I were both working with the International Bible Society to get thousands of copies of the Bible in the hands of people who didn't have them. Like King Saul and David, our lives could no longer remain separate; our paths would start to cross over and over again.

During this time, I experienced a bizarre vision/dream.

April 17, 2004

Thursday night I had a bizarre dream/vision while sleeping. I dreamed I was driving down the road (I guess in a convertible) and three books attached to one another blew into my arms. I think they turned out to be more like spiral-bound journals. I caught them so quickly in the dream it took me a while to process what they were and figure out they were my journals, I assume.

The second scene then is me going into my new friend's church and seeing the people taking stuff off the walls—awards, pictures, and accomplishments displayed. I later learned these were pictures of my new friend and his accomplishments. In the dream I don't know why this was happening, but it was.

The third scene was very simple but vivid. I caught the journals, and they spiraled around to the backside of the last journal, and in big black capital letters was the word HUMILITY. I have no idea what this dream means. I am confused, but I sense that the journal is from the Lord. I assume whatever the dream's timing, I need to be focused on HUMILITY.

I awoke very affected by the dream. I shared it with Tosha to see if it made any sense to her. She said it seemed like it was from God and that humility is the focal point.

I went back and looked at my journal from three years ago and, ironically enough, three years ago to date (exactly) I ask the Lord to do whatever necessary to keep me humble. I don't quite know what this means, but I take it as a sign from God. The past three years have been about God growing humility in my heart. I have missed God a number of times in the last three years, but He continues to shower me with His grace and lead me.

We had the International Bible Society meeting, and my new friend didn't show. Soon after this another nationally known leader started marriage conferences with my new friend to bolster the federal marriage amendment against homosexual marriages. The event had 3,200 people at my new friend's church with a simulcast to another 1,000 churches and 1,500 radio stations to hear this evening on marriage. The national leader with my new friend said that night our nation turned a moral corner in the fight against same-sex marriages.

I called Tosha after the broadcast. I told her about it. I told her it was confusing to me. God just keeps giving my new friend more authority and power. And now here is a nationally known Christian leader standing with my new friend over a marriage amendment against same-sex marriage when he himself struggles with homosexuality and has even confessed to me that he has more than likely done two or three things to disqualify him from ministry. I have no idea how he has been able to keep the lies secret for as long as he has. I so want to call the nationally known leader and tell him. How will it affect him when all of my new friend's lies come out? What is God doing? Would God allow this nationally known evangelical organization to make him president and then allow the nationally known leader to partner with him only to then expose him? Why? If yes, why?

As I listen to the nationally known leader's battle cry for Christians to fight, at the same time my devotions were leading me through Matthew where Jesus says the following to His disciples: "'Put away your sword,' Jesus told him. 'Those who use the sword will be killed by the sword. Don't you realize that I could ask my Father for thousands of angels to protect us, and he would send them instantly? But if I did how would the Scriptures be fulfilled that describe what must happen now?'" (Matthew 26:52).

God allows things to happen now so things can be fulfilled later. That is God's economy. My journal entry from that day continues . . .

The battle is not up to me, it is up to God. So the question is, how does He want me to fight for Him in His battle? Christians so often in our culture act like they are our only hope for preserving values.

Our city is so full of religious hypocrisy that it is not funny. I wonder when it will fall and burst open like Judas did?

In reference to my new friend, my devotions also led me through Mark 4. I believe these verses spoke to me about him: "Everything that is now hidden or secret will eventually be brought to light. Anyone who is willing to hear should listen and understand. And be sure to pay attention to what you hear. The more you do this, the more you will understand—and even more, besides. (Mark 4:22-24).

In the closing of this journal entry I wrote . . .

Last night Joshua pooped in the potty. It scared him to death, but he did it. We all cheered him on to victory. He was a very scared but happy little boy. Pooping in the potty is a huge deal for a boy. [He was 2.]

Why do I tell you this? Because in the midst of the "shameful" situations of our lives, life continues. Be sure not to miss them because you are fixated on the unresolved issues of your life. During this time God gave me Isaiah 50:7 to cling to as a promise: "But the Lord God helps me; therefore, I have not been disgraced; therefore I have set my face like a flint, and I know that I shall not be put to *shame*" (emphasis added). I trust You, Lord!

Trust means you don't demand an outcome from God. You trust the outcome will be good, because He *always* works everything to the *good* of those who love Him. Trust simply means, *I love You, Lord!* It's the part we play. Resist the shame and perceived defeat and trust Him, love Him, regardless. If you do, it will always end well. Even if it comes *after* death (Romans 8:28—an eternity with Him!).

I trust You, Lord!

SECRETS AND LIES

Human depravity is hard to crucify and harder to manage.

When our fourth born, Annalarie, was three years old, I was making our family breakfast. As I made the food, I sat it in front of them. I told her and her siblings, "Don't eat anything until we all sit down as a family to eat."

Annalarie said back to me from the breakfast table, "Dad, is licking eating?"

She's a funny girl who likes to push the boundaries, but don't we all from time to time?

As I write this chapter, I am listening to a song by Mary Lambert called "Secrets." One line in the song goes like this: "I don't care if the whole world knows what my secrets are." This is refreshing to consider and hopeful at best, but as I ask around, including to my teenage kids, I am reminded, it just isn't true.

No one honestly wants the *whole world* to know what their real secrets are. But I get the point: she doesn't want to live in a false way and pretend to be someone she is not—and that, I couldn't agree more with. We all need to live authentic, genuine, vulnerable, and honest lives if we hope to grow in real relationship with God and others.

However, all of us have secrets. I have secrets. You have secrets. Everyone you meet, love, talk to, live with, develop friendships with—and the list goes on—has secrets. And yes, we think we wouldn't mind if the whole world knew all our secrets, but that's just not true, nor is it healthy.

My experience has been that a person who is willing to tell a total stranger all the deepest secrets of their life with no relationship in return is usually a very sick person emotionally. They are grasping for relationship from anyone and everyone. They are willing to take unhealthy risks to get anyone to love them. Exposing all your secrets to someone you just met is the equivalent of being willing to give someone you just met at a coffee shop your bank account numbers and passwords to your financial accounts. It just isn't wise, and more than likely it will further perpetuate pain and sorrow in your life greater than you already have.

Trust is earned. It is given, not taken or demanded. Trust is not something you have to give away to "prove" to people you are worthy. Trust is what will naturally happen between two people when they take the time to build a relationship born out of real life. Over time, trust gives us the emotional deposits in our hearts to take the risks and share the real us with others. It is OK for people to have to earn the right to know all of who you are.

Yet, secrets that no one in your life knows about are equally damaging to your life as well.

I remember reading a book by my new friend, and one of the first quotes of the book that stood out to me was this: "Live as if there are no secrets." At first this statement seems noble, but as you press into it, you need to realize—we *all* have secrets. And secrets are *not* always wrong. Yes, sin is always wrong, but secrets can be right or wrong, depending on the nature of them.

I can have a secret that I bought my wife a special gift, and no one knows about it but me. That is OK, and she loves secrets like that by the way. I hate secrets. I don't like surprises. I do better with everything out in front of me, but she likes being surprised with secrets. This is a good thing!

Secrets are bad when they are kept to the harm of others or yourself. Proverbs 9:17 says, "Stolen water is sweet, and bread eaten in secret is pleasant." These kinds of secrets are fun. The juicier the better! But they are also devastating in time. Proverbs 9:18 says, "But he [the secret keeper] does not know that the dead are there, that her guests are in the depths of Sheol."

Brené Brown says, "You are only as healthy as your secrets." I find that pastors have lots of secrets. We keep a lot of secrets for people, but we ourselves often do not share our secrets. We keep them locked away with everyone else's secrets.

I have found this to be very damaging to the health of a leader or individual who is responsible for the lives of others. The enemy eventually uses these sorts of matters to trip them (us) up and this eventually causes great devastation.

As I write this chapter, another prominent leader has fallen in the Christian community due to secrets he kept and secrets others kept for him so that he could maintain his "charisma" and "ministry." They wanted to protect him, but eventually you can't even protect someone from their own secrets; eventually they begin to destroy the very fabric of the relationships that were established, and they erode the capacity for trust and alienate everyone eventually involved. It is a sad reality to watch and an even sadder reality to reconcile.

Isaiah 47:10 records this spirit of secrecy: "You felt secure in your wickedness, you said, 'No one sees me'; your wisdom and your knowledge led you astray, and you said in your heart, 'I am, and there is no one besides me.'" Wicked secrets make us arrogant, every time. Isaiah 47:11 speaks of this: "But evil shall come upon you, which you will not know how to charm away; disaster shall fall upon you, for which you will not be able to atone; and ruin shall come upon you suddenly, of which you know nothing."

Why do wicked secrets make us arrogant? Because wickedness kept to ourselves alienates us from God and God's people. It leaves us simply to the ploys of the enemy, and we are left to function like the enemy does. It is a very sad reality to watch when God's leaders start acting and functioning like the enemy of God does yet continue to claim the name of Jesus for their gain.

So, is there any hope for being able to live with healthiness in our secrets? Are we destined to be unhealthy in this area, or can we have balance and freedom in our secrets?

I think it is possible to live in health in the midst of our secrets but recognize that the enemy wants us to be secure in our secret keeping and even in how we expose our secrets. We must always live with a level of tension in this area of our lives that we are in need of a Savior 24/7. We can never wander far from God's grace and expect to live to tell about righteous happenings. Romans makes it really clear that we are a part of Christ. So whatever I share with you has to be lived in Christ, or even these tips and techniques will leave us squandering the precious time and relationships of our lives.

With that said, I want to share with you how I deal with the secrets of my life. And yes, I have secrets. I live knowing I have secrets, and I live knowing everyone else has secrets too. The question isn't, *Do you have secrets?* The question is, *Does anyone know about them? And do you have a way of letting people know about your secrets?*

Back in 1990 when I met Tosha at Liberty University, she taught me to journal. I had no idea at the time what journaling was. I was a freshman in college, and I was trying to get a grip on my personal purity. She challenged me to journal my thoughts and to record Scripture that would help me fight the attacks of the evil one.

One summer back in the '90s I went off to Florida to serve as a youth intern in a church. I had no idea what I was getting myself into.

As I left Virginia that summer, Tosha sent a pocket journal with me with lots of Scripture written inside of it. She challenged me to record my summer experiences in that pocket journal.

As a nineteen-year-old man, I was continuing to wrestle through my purity and making sure I was walking in practical, everyday holiness.

Soon after arriving, I was thrown quickly into a maze of challenges. I was personally battling for sexual purity in my own life, and I wasn't as wise then as I am now. (I could still use some growth in this area today, for the record.)

I dealt with attractions, temptations, and the secrets of others. I remember one day, the youth pastor I was interning under called me into his office. He asked me to close the door and said, "I need to tell you a secret."

I could see from the look on his face, he was distraught. I said, "OK, what is it?"

He said, "I think I am the Antichrist."

I studied his face for a good twenty seconds and finally concluded this was not a joke—he meant it. I said to him, "Who else knows this?"

He said, "Nobody."

I felt the even greater weight of this moment. I didn't know what to do as a nineteen-year-old with such a secret, but looking back, I know this is not the best way to handle a secret. You don't tell your secrets to total strangers. You don't tell your secrets to people you just met. You have to have a process, a way to go about chronicling the truth of your life so that it doesn't sneak up on you and others and destroy you like it did the youth pastor I was interning under. Eventually the truth came out, and there was more than just this secret he was carrying—he had a myriad of secrets in his family, marriage, and friendships. The devastation was great for that church, and I was keenly reminded again that you can't keep secrets; they will eventually catch up to you.

I decided that summer that journaling would be my way of telling all my secrets. I decided I would not wait until I was so desperate that I would tell anyone.

So, in the summer of 1990, I started journaling the truth of my life. I started recording my temptations, my trials, and my triumphs. I started listing in detail the good and bad of my life. It has become a documentary to me that I go back and re-read over and over again to gain perspective on myself and the challenges of my life. Without my journals I am not sure I could have written this book. I couldn't remember all these details without my journals.

During our dating years, I would record my temptations and my challenges. I didn't share them with Tosha because she wasn't my wife. However, as we neared engagement and eventually marriage, we each made a commitment to each other to live with full-disclosure about the triumphs and the temptations of our lives. I have been journaling now for over two decades, and I still don't *enjoy* putting my sins down on paper. I have things in writing that I am ashamed of and are very embarrassing to me. I have things that I wish were not true of my past, but they are, and I can't change my past—but neither do I need to be fully defined by it.

In the twenty-five years of our marriage, I have had times that I have needed to share with Tosha "my secrets." None were more painful than in 1999, two years into the church plant.

We finally got a chance to get away and recover from the intense fatigue we felt from two-plus years of church planting. We drove for a long time and stopped off at a campground in the mountains. We dug our small tent out of the Trooper, and we set it up by this little creek. I grabbed my new book by Phillip Yancey called *Finding God in Unexpectant Places*. I was so desperate as I read that book; I hoped to find God in that unexpected place, but I also kept telling myself, *I am never going back to that church.*

We eventually made our way to Yellowstone. We enjoyed some time there and in other nearby states. One time we stopped off just outside of Boulder at a place that allowed us to have a dog in our room. We grabbed the keys and noticed the movie selection in the lobby area. We picked out the movie *Horse Whisperer.*

We made our way up the stairs and into our room. Tosha was tired. She rested. I took the dog and went out to a picnic table by the hotel. I sat outside and began to journal. Never in a million years would I have dreamed that what was in my heart was in my heart. As I wrote, I discovered an emotional attraction to a woman other than my wife. It was humiliating. It was crushing to me, and I knew it would be to Tosha as well. I finished journaling, weeping, praying, and returned to the room.

We watched the movie. As God would have it, the movie was about a man and woman who were attracted to each other, but not married. They never spoke of it, but you could tell from the movie that they felt it. At the end of the movie, they chose not to act on those feelings. I turned to Tosha when the movie was over, and I felt like the Lord said, *Share your journal with her, NOW!*

I believe if I would have said no on that day, I may never have written this book and my marriage would have never made it to two-plus decades. Secrets are that powerful and that destructive.

I gave her my journal. She read it. I watched as she began to weep. It crushed me. It humiliated me. *I needed every second of it.* What kind of guy finds himself attracted to another woman when his wife is seven months pregnant with their second child?

Me.

That moment propelled me to a two-year accountability with my friend Vance who God used to spare my life tremendous heartache. (He was also one of the two elders who walked with me through many situations.) He helped me build safeguards in this area of my life. I am very grateful for Vance's friendship in my life. I learned, in my flawed faithfulness, from Vance how to share my secrets with people who have earned my trust.

Vance would say to me over and over again, "You won't pull this [this being living a lifetime of flawed faithfulness for God] off without dependence on others." I learned that *no one can handle their secrets alone.* I can't. Vance couldn't. My new friend couldn't. You can't.

Looking back, if I hadn't started journaling my secrets in 1990, I would have never had a chance to even share my secrets with Tosha in 1999.

The disciplines you start today may yield little to no fruit early on, but if they are continued over time, they may be the very things that save your life, your marriage, and your ministry. They may be the very things that give you the courage to discern God's voice and what and who He wants you to share it with in your life. What you do determines who you become when it comes to spiritual disciplines.

Little did Tosha know, she would teach me a discipline that would save both us and our marriage.

Since that time, I have made another commitment. I have decided that when each of my children turn twenty years old, I will give them a copy of that corresponding year of my life. My oldest is almost twenty. Can you hear that? That's my knees knocking. As fearful as that commitment makes me, I want them to see what I was like then at their age—the good, the bad, and the everything in between. I want it to give them hope too and for them to know they can't handle their secrets alone.

Moms and dads, it is not the secrets of our past that we keep from our kids that will determine the success of our lives. It is the secrets we share at the appointed time. And yes, our secrets shared may very well be the key to the success of theirs!

The difference I see between me and my new friend is I don't "live as if there are no secrets." I share my secrets with my wife and others to get help before I self-destruct. You can do the same.

Honestly, I don't want the whole world to know all my secrets. But guess what? They don't have to or need to. What method will you use to make sure those who need to know your secrets, do?

THE FLEECE

H ey, Kelly. I think I found your dream property. You need to
check it out.

This is what one of the elders, Bob, at the church I pastor
said to me over a decade ago in 2005. My family and I had moved
into a brand-new house just a few years prior. We had finished the
basement, and we had every intention of living in this house for a
decade until we were in our forties. Then we hoped to get some land
and animals so we could teach our kids the lessons we learned from
the animals in our lives as kids.

We decided to just go *look*. Turned out we knew the real estate
agent and felt comfortable calling her and letting her know this
property was out of our league, but we wanted to honor our elder's
suggestion and take a look at it.

Looking back, we don't know how this happened, but even
though the property was in major disarray, we fell in love with it. We
were smitten. Instantly we told ourselves, "We can't afford this."

I was challenged to put down on paper the obstacles that
we had to overcome to purchase and then see what happened. We
knew the price was out of our reach. We knew we couldn't buy the
property without a loan, and we knew we couldn't buy the property
without selling our existing home for a good price.

How do you know when God is in something? How do you know when God is directing you or you are just directing yourself? Well, let's eliminate some of the conversations and decisions from this equation. Here are a few questions to ask yourself:

1. Does what you want to do line up with Scripture, or is it contradictory to Scripture? (What verses are you focused on in making this decision?)

2. When you pray about it, what type of feeling and perspective do you get from the Holy Spirit?

3. What do your friends/family who walk with the Lord think about it?

If the decision can make it through this gauntlet, now what? Does it mean you should do it? Well, not yet.

Sometimes understanding the divine Creator's voice in our lives seems to be an impossibility. Don't get me wrong, I can hear the voice of God in my mind, but I very seldom know what He means by what He says—even less so, when it will occur. I miss God's timing *a lot*!

Most people I know, if they are honest, have a very difficult time discerning the voice of God in their lives over all the other voices in their lives, including their own. So if something is not illegal, unbiblical, or unethical, how do you know if you should do it or not?

Fear is a very real companion during times like this. My friend Joel says, "If you don't want to do something, then as a believer, that's probably God." But still, how do you know if it is God speaking to you?

If the thing that you feel compelled to do is not illegal, unbiblical, or unethical, how do you discern if it is God telling you to do it? Judges 6 records the call of Gideon. It was during a time when it was difficult to hear from God—signs and wonders were not prevalent. However, abuse at the hands of the Midianites was very prevalent.

The angel of the Lord came to Gideon and called him to save his people from the abuse of Midian. Gideon was scared to death.

He wanted to be obedient, but he didn't want to die. Can't blame him!

Once God had eliminated all of Gideon's excuses for obeying and leading his people to freedom, Gideon asked for a fleece. What is a fleece? The technical definition is "the coat of wool shorn from a sheep."[6] Gideon wanted to make sure God had spoken to him beyond any doubt. So he took a piece of shorn wool from a sheep and said to the Lord,

> "If you will save Israel by my hand, as you have said, behold, I am laying a fleece of wool on the threshing floor. If there is dew on the fleece alone, and it is dry on all the ground, then I shall know that you will save Israel by my hand, as you have said." And it was so. When he rose early the next morning and squeezed the fleece, he wrung enough dew from the fleece to fill a bowl with water. Then Gideon said to God, "Let not your anger burn against me; let me speak just once more. Please let me test just once more with the fleece. Please let it be dry on the fleece only, and on all the ground let there be dew." And God did so that night; and it was dry on the fleece only, and on all the ground there was dew. (Judges 6:36-40)

After that, the term *fleece* biblically took on a dual or double meaning. Some critics would say you have the Word of God, prayer, God's church, and the Holy Spirit—you don't need fleeces. I disagree. Fleeces should not contradict the above means to accomplishing or discerning God's will but neither do they have to be left out of the equation. In Acts 1 the apostles needed to pick Judas's replacement. Look at how they went about it:

> "So one of the men who have accompanied us during all the time that the Lord Jesus went in and out among us, beginning from the baptism of John until the day when he was taken up from us—one of these men must become with us a witness to his resurrection." And they put forward two, Joseph called Barsabbas, who was also called Justus, and Matthias. And they prayed and said, "You,

---

6. A combination of dictionary.com and the Oxford English Dictionary's definition.

Lord, who knows the hearts of all, show which one of these two you have chosen to take the place in this ministry and apostleship from which Judas turned aside to go to his own place." And they cast lots for them, and the lot fell on Matthias, and he was numbered with the eleven apostles. (Acts 1:21-26)

Did you catch that? They cast lots in verse 26. They did the equivalent of drawing straws to determine who the new twelfth apostle should be. In essence, they cast a fleece—the twelve apostles who had been used by Jesus to perform miracles. To me, a fleece is simply a divine, intentional coincidence.

Once you have gone through the disciplines mentioned above, it is important to make sure you have heard correctly. What do I mean by this? Let me illustrate through the circumstances of the property we were thinking of buying. We decided there were three things that had to happen for us to *know* God wanted us to do this. First, we had a limit we were willing to pay for the purchase of the property. Second, a family member would have to help us with the purchase because it was out of our league. Third, there was a minimum limit we were willing to take for our existing house. We figured if these three things would line up, then we would take it as signs from God that we should do this.

Our offering price and the asking price of the property was more than one hundred thousand dollars apart. We thought we were safe in this process.

We made our offer. We were not even close to what they wanted. To make a long story short, they said no. I remember the anxiety I felt from that experience. I remember the real estate agent calling and saying they would not even remotely take what we had offered. We were crushed and disappointed but relieved at the same time. We were relieved to know that it wasn't the Lord's will for us, so we moved on, or at least began the process. The emotional residual would take time.

Three days later, the real estate agent called back. "Good news, the owners said they have not been able to sleep for three days and have decided to take your offer."

We went from crushed and disappointed to overly exuberant— to absolutely terrified. What have we done? What have we gotten ourselves into?

We called our family member and told them about this transaction, secretly hoping they wouldn't help us. They gave us exactly what we needed to purchase the home. Two fleeces completed, one to go!

We not only had to sell our house for a minimum amount, but we had to sell it within a limited time or the deal on the other property would expire. We were actually able to find someone willing to buy the house in the time allotted, but they wanted us to make repairs to a house that was practically brand new. Besides the principle of it, we knew we had to get a certain amount out of our house or we knew that this was not God's will for us. (And by the way, it is not about sin or not sin in this decision but wisdom and obeying and following God's leading—not ours.)

I called the real estate agent back and said, "We can't pay for those expenses or we will go below what we have agreed is wise, and so we have to say no."

The agent said to me, "Are you willing to lose this sort of a deal over two thousand dollars?"

I said, "I know this may not make any sense, but we have put out fleeces, and we aren't willing to do the deal even if it was one penny." I said, "This is how we know God wants us to do this, otherwise we are going to assume He doesn't."

The agent was a bit frustrated with me, but she said, "Let me see what I can do." In less than fifteen minutes she called back and said, "The deal is done." I said, "How?" She said, "I decided to pay for it."

Yes, humanly speaking you can explain away every one of these "fleeces" as coincidence or some form of massaging the process, but we believe that after you have walked through the spiritual disciplines, if God fulfills your fleeces, He gives you the freedom to choose.

We have learned over and over again that *flawed faithfulness depends upon fleeces to know what God wants us to do from time to time in our lives.* We are very grateful for these three fleeces because the first five to seven years we lived at the property we regretted more than we enjoyed living there. Everything on the property was broken, and we were overwhelmed with what to do about it. However, we have in the last few years began to see the benefits for our kids that has come from living at the property. We moved there for the sake of our kids, and we have stayed there because the fleeces gave us the confidence that regardless of how difficult it has been, it is what He wants for us.

Let me reiterate again: be careful using this plan for things you want to do and are just looking for a way to justify it. It is important that the well-being of someone other than just yourself is going to benefit from this process.

In case you need a second opinion, let me tell you another story that impacted our lives—another time when we used a fleece to discern His direction for our lives. It had to do with our fifth child, Journey Grace.

We had four kids, and both of us were struggling with our health along with the property we were living on. When we were in college, I had a dream/vision of Tosha and I sitting around a dining room table with five kids. The birth order was girl, boy, girl, twin boys. However, at this time, we only had four kids, and the birth order was girl, girl, boy, girl, and only God knew it would be that way. Because the details of the dream regarding the genders of our children was not accurate, I felt the freedom to say that the dream was not of God. However, Tosha did not agree. She felt like we were to have five kids. We always said, "Four pregnancies, five kids," but that didn't come true. Life has a way of *not* coming true the way you planned it or dreamed it to be. When this occurs, we all tend to let ourselves off the hook on things that we don't want to do or don't have the energy or courage to do, like Gideon.

For over a year we battled to figure this out in our marriage. Finally, we agreed to set a fleece date with God, and if no baby was conceived by such a date, we would take that as a sign that God wanted us to be done birthing kids.

The date came, August 1, 2005, and went—no baby. We were sad, but we felt we had God's answer. Actually, I was sad but more relieved because of our health issues, the pressures of ministry and life, the raising of four kids, and the challenges of where we lived.

I wanted to know we were done with pregnancy, diapers, and the terrible twos. I was sad because it seemed like it just wasn't right.

A few days later, Tosha and I had a date night. We watched a movie, and God blessed us with a special and unique time of connection as a married couple. We experienced the Holy Spirit in our intimacy unlike anything before or after. As they say, "the rest is history." Nine months later, Journey Grace Williams, our fifth child, was born. Because we were unsure of a fifth child at this point, we believe God divinely orchestrated the circumstances, and His presence confirmed in a special way that though we had sincerely sought Him, we had missed it, and He was still in control of the final outcomes of our lives. This is hugely comforting to us even today.

Fleeces are tools to guide our decisions, not control them. Fleeces are used to make wisdom and judgment decisions, not moral and ethical decisions—the Bible does that. We are grateful God saw fit to override our decision-making process and fulfill His will for our lives in spite of our fleece.

Every time I look at our property, I am reminded of the fleeces we used to determine we should buy it. Every time I look at Journey Grace, I am reminded of the exception we made to our fleece, and I am grateful for both. At the end of the day, rest in this: The Bible is very clear—if you are sincerely seeking God, you will find Him one way or the other. Keep pressing in, and don't be afraid of the Gideon fleece! It is a part of the flawed faithful life. Use it from time to time to figure out what God wants you to do with the details of your life.

"Randomly Ordered" Encounters

How can something be ordered and seemingly random at the same time? Perspective is everything.

Paul says in 1 Corinthians 13:12, "For now we see in a mirror dimly, but then face to face. Now I know in part; then I shall know fully, even as I have been fully known." There is debate over when this will take place in a person's life and how. Nevertheless, there is no debate over whether we *all* experience this perspective in our lives.

Life is confusing, regardless of how godly you are or how well you can hear the divine Creator's voice speak to you through His Word. We are all left to look for patterns and designs in our lives to give us hope that the divine Creator of our lives not only sees our lives, but He is involved in the details of our everyday lives.

We all lose hope. I have lost hope so many times it is not even funny, and without fail, these "randomly ordered" encounters help me push on—not knowing the outcome or the reason, but nonetheless confirming that they are real and that they matter.

Now I don't believe they are independent of our pursuit of God through His Word, His church, or His Spirit. We can't stop pursuing God through these means because of woundedness, laziness, or confusion. These patterns are revealed to us as we labor in these known arenas that enable us to hear God's voice better.

As we read God's Word, fellowship with His people, and pray in the Spirit for understanding, the random nature of these ordered encounters is like daily supplements we take to help us get through the day. We can't live off of them spiritually, but we equally can't do what God has asked us to do without them. They give us the extra energy we need to push through those hard days, weeks, and seasons of our lives.

Proverbs 2:3 says, "Make your ear attentive to wisdom and incline your heart to understanding." God's Word is not going to tell you everything you need to know about your life. I know, I just became a heretic for saying that. But trust me, I doubt you will meet anybody who reads their Bible any more than I do. When I was eighteen years old I made a daily commitment to read the Bible, ten chapters a day. I am presently on my eightieth reading of the Bible. I crave the Bible more than random signs, but I also know that the Bible does not get down into the tall weeds of the details of my life. *But God's presence and His voice does.*

When Martin Luther confronted the church, he was attempting to give back to the people the ability to hear from God on their own. Every day of a believer's life should be centered around this idea of looking for God in the details of their lives as they practice the spiritual disciplines of prayer, Scripture reading, and even possibly journaling.

God asked me to do something I didn't have the courage to do, and after I did it, I wasn't sure God even asked me to do it because of how it turned out. It is normal to doubt. It is normal to question. *I hope this book makes it normal to look for God in the details of our lives,* so we can know God is in them, cheering us on to victory for doing what He asked us to do.

During this long season of my life, I doubted a lot. I looked around at my life, my new friend's life, and wondered aloud to myself often. The *coincidences* were becoming daily. I couldn't escape him in my daily life, regardless of how hard I tried. Somehow, someway, the situation would rear its ugly head, and I would plummet once again into the abyss of confusion. Anger was my constant companion, and I struggled to shake it.

During this season I begged God to spare my new friend and to help him repent. I asked the Lord to show mercy on him. I wanted this story to end well—and soon.

Nothing changed.

During this time, a piece came out that portrayed him as one of the most influential evangelical leaders ever. I didn't know how to handle this. I went from begging God for mercy on him to wondering if God sees the injustices of this world, and more importantly, does He care?

Proverbs 28 was given to me often in this season of my life. It was a comfort and a torture to me: "Evil men do not understand justice, but those who seek the Lord understand it completely. Better is a poor man who walks in his integrity than a rich man who is crooked in his ways. . . . Whoever conceals his transgressions will not prosper, but he who confesses and forsakes them will obtain mercy. . . . *Whoever rebukes a man will afterward find more favor than he who flatters with his tongue*" (Proverbs 28:5-6, 13, 23, emphasis added).

Verse 23 is the one that stood out to me the most over and over again. The "coincidence" that this was "23" was God's reminder to me through His ordered Word and through this "random" number that He saw and was involved in the outcome of this ordeal. It is Scripture combined with the "random" that gave me hope. It was a promise I held on to for two reasons: (1) because it is in God's Word, and (2) it was tied to the random reoccurring events of my life.

It was tailored for my time. It was given to me over and over again in various ways for four-plus years. I can't tell you how many times I lost hope in this season. Our fourth born, Annalarie, started suffering with seizures. It took me back to the depths of despair, as I remembered the fear I felt from losing my mom to a drunk driver.

Another passage that became a staple in this season was Psalm 27: "Though an army encamp against me, my heart shall not fear; though war arise against me, yet I will be confident. . . . Hear, O Lord, when I cry aloud; be gracious to me and answer me! You have said, 'Seek my face.' My heart says to you, 'Your face, Lord, do I seek.' Hide not your face from me. Turn not your servant away in anger, O you who have been my help. Cast me not off; forsake me not, O God of my salvation!" (Psalm 27:3, 7-9).

That same year, a prominent paper published an article on my new friend that touted him as a man of God with real influence, power, and sway. It angered me greatly. *Lord, do You see?* In Psalm 37 it says, "Refrain from anger. . . . For the evildoers shall be cut off. . . . I have been young, and now am old, yet I have not seen the righteous forsaken. . . . For the Lord loves justice; he will *not* forsake his saints" (Psalm 37:8-9, 25, 28, emphasis added).

The randomness went silent for about six months. Then on April 23, 2006, of all the numbered days it could have been, I began the process of launching a new pastor's network with a leader at a Christian organization of which I was a member. How can something be divinely ordered and random at the same time? I didn't plan it, but there it is: April 23. The random nature of that number showed up in this story over and over and over again. I wouldn't have picked it, and I still don't understand it, but now looking back, I embrace it.

Just because something is random doesn't mean it isn't divinely ordered. It is a matter of perspective. "I have been young, and now I am old, yet I have not seen the righteous forsaken."

The randomness of *23* isn't a substitute for the ordered things like God's Word, but neither is it to be ignored. They sometimes work in tandem with one another. I have learned that *flawed faithfulness gains confidence in God's voice through repeated and seemingly random physical patterns*—like *23* in conjunction with His ordered Word, the Bible.

God is speaking to *every one of us* on a *daily basis* through the ordered and the seemingly random, and it is my hope that this book gives you hope to look for the patterns that are "randomly ordered" for your benefit. I didn't see them then, but I see them now, and I pray this gives you hope that, like the psalmist, I too have never seen the righteous forsaken.

Thank You, Lord, for the "randomly ordered" encounters. They grow my confidence in You.

Section 3:
The Countdown

3:21 A.M.

I t began again for the final time at 3:21 a.m.

    The "awakening" experiences started again in the night. It would prove to be the final round of *23* experiences. Relief was on the way. The weight of the burdens I felt for this situation had reached epic portion, and my heart was growing numb to the voice of God.

    I had already lost hope in my journals at this point. No longer did I record these "random" nighttime experiences. I was numb to them. I had learned to see the time as a corresponding Scripture God wanted me to read, but I even gave up on that. The weight of the burdens I felt for this situation overwhelmed me.

    I woke up often at 3:21 a.m., and I went to the bathroom. In the dark I heard the words, "The time is now." I felt the end of this turmoil was near, but I had been wrong so many times regarding the timing that I refused to believe I was hearing the voice of God speak to me.

    As I look back on this, I see the number *23* in this equation, and I see that God was using this to let me know the countdown was on and the end was near.

    Psalm 32:1-2 says: "Blessed is the one whose transgression is forgiven, whose sin is covered. Blessed is the man against whom the Lord counts no iniquity and in whose spirit there is no *deceit*" (emphasis added). I know this is taking it far, but stay with me. The number *32* (from the Psalms reference) is the inverse of *23*. This *32* is what God has to do to us when we won't let His favor lead us to repentance. Numbers 32:23 says, "Be sure and know your sins will find you out." I am implying here with Psalm 32 that it is the opposite of Psalm 23. Psalm 23 is about God's favor; Psalm 32 is about His judgment. When we won't respond to His favor, (i.e., His conviction of the Spirit and our willingness to be led by His rod and staff, then He has to judge us to get our attention. He has to expose our sin to bring us to repentance.

Unfortunately, this is extremely painful and rarely works because when our sin is exposed publicly instead of us confessing privately, it leads to us hardening our hearts and even looking for reasons why we are justified in our actions. All throughout the Old Testament God tells Israel that they wouldn't listen, and when we don't listen to all the channels of accountability provided for us in the church and our families, then He is left with no choice but to bring the pagan world in to judge us. This happens to Israel over and over again—the Assyrians, Babylonians, and so forth and so on.

What I am trying to say is that humiliation at this point appeared to be the only means left to try and get my new friend's attention. It didn't have to be this way, but it was sadly the only way he would listen. This can become true for all of us if we don't listen to the layers of accountability God has for our lives. Deceit was my new friend's companion, and public humiliation, sadly, was the only solution to his deceit.

I grieved a thousand deaths in that season, but I also begged and begged God to bring it to light because I did not know how much longer I could bear up under the weight of the burden that had been on me now for almost six years.

August 22, 2006

I continue to battle the heavy demons that weigh on me at this time. I feel this time to be a very difficult time and potentially divisive in many ways. I feel at times a lot of anxiety and potential frustration because of the confusion. It is difficult to discern the proper process. I learned even more sad news yesterday of how my new friend leads his church. It saddens me and angers me. Oh, Lord, can it be over soon?

I found myself begging You this morning in prayer to expose the darkness and tear down the stronghold. I beg You again, Lord, to make Yourself known, and I cringe as I ask, but I ask, bring Your hand of judgment upon us, Your people. Let us not live a lie. Show us why sin matters to You, because I watch my new friend's life and leadership, thinking, "What difference does it make? Does it really matter how you live?" I am losing hope as I know many others are, God.

I beg You, please reveal Yourself to me at least in this situation today. Lord, I did what You asked me to do, and I now suffer for it. I want to be willing to suffer for it. I want to be willing to suffer more, but I don't know how much more I can take. I fear what I may do. I fear trying to take matters into my own hands. I don't want it to be me against "the man." I want it to be You (God) revealing Yourself to me, to us.

I feel like the Lord said "Psalm 32:8." The Lord says, "I will guide you along the best pathway for your life. I will advise you and watch over you." My heart takes courage, but I am not comforted. Lord, I must confess (I guess), I am angry. I want justice in this situation with "the man." I want to be vindicated. I want the truth to come out. Do You want to use me to bring it out? I feel like You are saying "yes." Would You confirm it to me in Your Word?

I feel like the Lord gave me Psalm 58:10-11: "The godly will rejoice when they see injustice avenged. They will wash their feet in the blood of the wicked. Then at last everyone will say, 'There truly is a reward for those who live for God; surely there is a God who judges justly here on earth.'"

Lord, forgive me for my arrogance, but I am desperate. When are You going to judge justly in "the man's" situation? When, oh God, are You going to vindicate me? I can't take this anymore, God. I am falling to pieces. I am consumed by the injustice and baffled by Your silence.

Rescue me so that I know how to rescue others. Show me that justice matters in this world so that I live my life caring about justice for others. I am so close to giving up. God, it scares me. When I give up, I sin. The stakes are high now.

I feel like the Lord gave me Psalm 63:9, 11: "But those plotting to destroy me will come to ruin. They will go down into the depths of the earth. . . . Liars will be silenced." God, will You silence "the man" today?

I feel like the Lord gave me Psalm 73:

"Truly God is good to Israel, to those whose hearts are pure. But as for me I came so close to the edge of the cliff! My feet were slipping, and I was almost gone. For I envied the proud when I saw them prosper despite their wickedness. . . . These fat cats have everything their hearts could ever wish for! They scoff and speak only evil; in their pride they seek to crush others. . . . And so the people are dismayed and confused [that is me], drinking in all their words. 'Does God realize what is going on?' they ask. . . . Was it for nothing that I kept my heart pure and kept myself from doing wrong?

So I tried to understand why the wicked prosper. But what a difficult task it is! Then one day I went into your sanctuary, O God, and I thought about the destiny of the wicked. . . . Then I realized how bitter I had become, how pained I had been by all I had seen. I was so foolish and ignorant. . . . You will keep on guiding me. Whom have I in heaven but You? . . . Those who desert God perish [paraphrase], but as for me, how good it is to be near God! I have made the Sovereign Lord my shelter and I will tell everyone about the wonderful things you do" (Psalm 73:1-3, 7-8, 10-11, 13, 16-17, 21-22, 24-25, 27-28).

Help me, Lord, to do this! I still beg You, Lord, when will You remove him? Psalm 82:1 says, "God presides over heaven's court; he pronounces judgment on the judges [the leaders]."

Lord, would You bring Your judgment today, even if it requires sacrifice on my part? I cringe in asking, but I believe the request is of You. Will You bring it today? Will you give a Scripture to know I am on the right path or not?

I feel like the Lord gave me 2 Chronicles 24. The only time mentioned in there is verse 23: "At the beginning of the year." I take this to mean that at the beginning of the year, the judgment will begin.

Am I hearing You right, Lord? I feel like He gave me Proverbs 8:9: "My words are plain to anyone with understanding, clear to those who want to learn." I want to learn! I take this as from God. Proverbs 12:1 says, "To learn, you must love discipline." Discipline here is correction. Correct me, Lord. I am Your child.

I learned *life begins to make sense again with God when He exposes unrepentant sin.* No fun, but necessary.

Two and half months later, the day of reckoning finally came.

A SPIRITUAL 9/11

E ventually God reconciles injustices and vindicates wrongs. Romans 12:19 says, "Beloved, *never* avenge yourselves, but leave it to the wrath of God, for it is written, 'Vengeance is mine says the Lord, I will take it.'"

Journal Entry
November 5, 2006

The day of reckoning has finally come regarding the situation with "the man." After nearly six years, broadcast and print media broke a story about "the man" paying a gay prostitute for sex. He reportedly also purchased and supposedly took meth. He denied it all but then on Friday confessed to the meth but said he didn't take it. He also confessed to knowing the man [prostitute] and getting a massage from him. Then yesterday around 3 p.m. I learned that he had been fired.

My head, heart, and guts have been spinning and churning for the past three days. I can't believe it is over. I told a local paper that this is a spiritual 9/11 for the evangelical community.

Today they will be reading a letter from my new friend and his wife.

How do I feel? I feel everything. I feel primarily grief and sadness. I feel at times confusion, chaos, relief, peace, freedom, hope, bitterness, anger, frustration, hurt, anxiety, sorrow, anxiousness, a sense of being overwhelmed, and eagerness to lead.

I learned from this that life begins to make sense again with God, when He vindicates wrongs done to you and others. I see God's hand. It is crystal clear. I hear His voice clearer than ever—above all the before-mentioned emotions that were sabotaging my senses. I feel somewhat like I did when mom was killed. My mind is racing constantly. I woke up replaying all the thoughts.

I remember him saying to me in the Wal-Mart parking lot when I pulled up to confront him, he said, jokingly, "Did you bring the drugs?" If he was joking then, he isn't anymore.

I remember his wife saying to my face, "We have a great sexual relationship."

I remember one of the members of the board calling for my repentance after the hotel meeting with his presbytery. I remember wailing like a baby after he soundly defeated me in that hotel conference room with his wife and independent counsel (assumingly) by his side.

I remember that same board member coming to me later to tell me I was right, and he wanted to ask me for forgiveness.

I remember Vance and the elder team holding me back from saying or doing things later I would regret. If it hadn't been for them, I would have blown it.

I remember him confessing to me.

God protected me all these times. It is over. He is removed. I want to contact him. I want to help him. I also want closure for myself, but I may never get it. I have so many questions for him.

The Sunday after this all came out, I confronted it head on. I didn't mention my role, because how do you? I just said to our church, "'The man's' sin is in the newspaper, but ours isn't. Let his sin sober us to our sin. He can't hide his anymore, but we still can. James 5:17 tells us it is important to confess to God for forgiveness and to confess to others for healing."

In the days that followed this day of reckoning, I battled greatly with pride. The enemy has a way of beating us down and telling us we are nothing, and then when something happens in our lives that erases his ability to use this against us, he immediately turns and starts telling us, *You are actually really something.*

The urge to tell everybody my role in this was great. I knew (at the time and in this season) my motive for sharing would not be to help others, like I believe it is now, but to prop my ego up. This needed time to season and marinate in my heart. I needed to know for sure God wanted me to share this with others. After seventeen years and many answers to prayer, I believe now is the time. I am grateful though, because looking back, I was as accountable to my board then as I am now.

Sometime after it all broke and the dust settled, the chair of the presbytery was speaking at a conference I was attending, and I wanted to go see him. I wanted to have some closure with him.

I walked up to him after the service and we greeted one another. It had been almost six years since we had seen one another. I had changed more than he. I said to him, "You don't recognize me, do you?"

He said, "I don't."

I said, "I'm the young man who sat before the presbytery to try and help with 'the man.'"

He said, "I do remember you. You look a lot better with hair." (My head was shaved at the time of the meeting almost six years prior.) He said to me, "You know, I said to my wife many times, what if that young man was right?"

He prayed for me, and we parted ways. For the past eight-plus years I have had to process this without any real sense of closure. I have never spoken to my new friend in person since the ordeal. I called him right after it came out, but he quickly hung up on me. I texted him about this book, and he wanted no part in it.

We all have situations in our lives that, even when they are vindicated, they still don't make sense to us. We each have a backdrop to our lives that God uses to teach us about ourselves.

Still to this day, our nation doesn't fully understand 9/11 and the effect it has had on our nation. Still to this day, I don't understand the full effect that this spiritual 9/11 has had on me and many others. I walk with a limp because of it.

God is still a mysterious God to me. As God says to Isaiah, "my ways are higher than your ways and my thoughts [are] higher than your thoughts" (Isaiah 55:9). I don't understand why God governs and rules the world the way He does. As a pastor, I talk with scores of people who battle the same things. Making sense of all the circumstances in your life is a good goal, but I doubt it is attainable in this life. Even when situations eventually turn out the way you thought, hoped, or prayed they would, you still live with a lot of nagging questions that will leave you puzzled by the order and details of this life.

I had not seen my new friend since that dreadful spiritual 9/11. Then I went out to lunch with someone who found themselves victimized by this situation as well. He was on staff at the time at my new friend's church. He and I have known each other for years, but we have never spoken of the situation. He and I are now both pastors in the same city.

We talked briefly during our lunch, and he asked me if I had ever talked with my new friend since the last encounter. I told him I had not, nor had I even crossed paths with him or seen him. I said, "I know one day our paths will cross again, I just have no idea when that day will come."

Five hours after saying this, my new friend walked into the restaurant where I was on a date with my fourth born, Annalarie. I had no idea what to do, and I realized that spiritual 9/11 was still very fresh and raw in my life after thirteen years of processing it. He came within ten feet of me but wouldn't look up at me. The moment passed, and the sadness of the situation remains where I long to see that man redeemed.

Ten years after 9/11, our nation was able to hunt down Osama bin Laden. One of our Navy Seals was able to take out the most ruthless terrorist our nation had ever known. Justice had been served for all the families who lost loved ones on 9/11.

I am grateful that our nation was able to put an end to such a ruthless terrorist, but that day didn't heal the wounds that exist in the hearts of those who lost loved ones on that day. That day didn't mark the beginning of a new dawn for our nation. Grief is grief. Justice in this life can't stop grief, only redemption can. And redemption can only come from Jesus Christ, our Lord and Savior.

November 5, 2006, does not make it all "right" with me. I still long for the day when that spiritual 9/11 can become a fully redeemed story. And I can't redeem my new friend. I can't make him take responsibility for what he did or what he did to me. To this day, he still believes nobody tried to help him. I carry deeply within my person the sorrow that he still can't see that I tried to help him. I didn't want to destroy him. God didn't want to destroy him.

I long for the day when the day of reckoning can become a day of redemption, but sin has to be owned as sin before grace can be received. Redemption begins at confession because confession is what triggers God's grace.

First John 1:9 says, "If you confess your sins, he is faithful and just to forgive you and cleanse you from *all* unrighteousness." The word *sin* is in the plural in the original language. It is a willingness to acknowledge the specifics of our lives and forsake them in exchange for God's grace and redemption. I don't know if my new friend has ever, or will ever, acknowledge the sin in his life, but I have learned some valuable lessons from this spiritual 9/11 that I will take with me through the rest of the days of my existence upon this earth. God has used numbers to breathe into me a holy awareness of His sovereign power over all the details of my life.

I have to let go of trying to understand what God's will and goal was for "the man" and turn my attention to what He has shown me and how He has chosen to use this in my life. God *never* wastes pain. In His economy, "*all* things work together for good to them that love God, to them who are the called according to his purpose" (Romans 8:28 KJV). That verse tells me that if I keep loving God, He will redeem everything about my life, eventually.

I now have to turn my attention to seeing the good that came out of this spiritual 9/11 as opposed to just focusing on the brokenness that I can't do anything about. Unfortunately, the spiritual 9/11s in our lives and those whom we love are necessary to get our attention, but the day of redemption is far more important.

We all have situations in our lives that, even when they are vindicated, they still don't make full sense. Justice is important in this life, but it can't stop grief, only redemption can. It is important to seek redemption over justice. Like in the book of Genesis, Joseph went through a lot at the hands of his brothers, but at the end of the ordeal, he said, "What you meant for evil, God meant for good" (Genesis 50:20).

Let God bring the justice to the situations of your life. Make His redemption your focus for yourself and for others. This will cause life to make a lot more sense in the end and free you to truly live again.

NUMBERS 32:23

N umbers 32:23 says, "Be sure your sin will find you out."
Sometime after my new friend fell, a bizarre movie
called *The Number 23*, starring Jim Carrey, was released in theaters.
The movie is about a man who discovers an obscure book about
the number *23,* which leads him on a descent into darkness. As
he becomes more obsessed with its contents, he becomes more
convinced that it is, in fact, based on his life. To his horror, he
discovers grave consequences in store for the book's main character.

Numbers 32:23 becomes the central "text" of the movie.
Through this random book that Carrey finds, his character begins
to discover his sins. At the end of the movie, he is sentenced to
prison for his actions, and the movie ends with Numbers 32:23 on
the screen: "Be sure your sin will find you out."

Needless to say, this freaked me out a bit, having gone through
all this numerology during the stuff with my new friend. I am not a
conspiracy theory kind of person, but I do experience things that are
difficult for me to explain.

God used the number *23* to wake me numerous times during
these separate seasons of my life, spanning over a six-year period.
During that time, I couldn't have told you what Numbers 32:23
says, not because I hadn't read it numerous times but because this

experience had not shaped me like it has now. I got to watch a very private example of Numbers 32:23 play out on a very public stage. And though it grieves me, it also breathes into me a great appreciation for confession and a great awareness of harboring "secrets" from God.

I preach sermons anywhere from one hundred to one hundred fifty times a year. I am continually telling people to repent, to confess, to come clean with God, to say to Him the things He already knows about you. And over time it is easy to become consumed with helping everyone else with their sins, and I forget about the brokenness of my own life. It is a common mistake for pastors.

God told the nation of Israel that when they went into the land to not forget about Him. He told them they would drink from wells they didn't dig, eat from vineyards they didn't plant, and live in houses they didn't build. When God blesses our lives, the temptation is to think, *I deserve this.* If we give into this thought, our lives lead us down a path of destruction that we have a very difficult time coming back from.

See, when God blesses our lives, we are blessed. We are happy. We are thankful, but then the enemy comes along and says, "Look, look what you did." Now that is damaging, but what is more damaging is the next thing he says to us. He says, "Look, you deserve more."

See, in this life, if you are living just for God's blessings, they will never be enough. God can't bless you enough for you to stay happy. Why? Because it is not God's blessings that ultimately make us happy, it is God's character in us that makes us happy. If we are not becoming more like Jesus every day, then we are becoming less like Jesus every day. And if we are becoming less like Jesus every day, then His blessings get lost along the way, and somehow or another we think to ourselves that we did something to deserve them and thus we deserve more.

This "deserving of more" forces our hand to do something about it. However, all of us fall short of the glory of God, and when we have dedicated our lives to God, we can't be chasing after "more blessings we deserve" if we are confessing sin we regret. And so, what is a person to do?

They stop confessing. Why? Because they have convinced themselves, like the main character in the movie *The Number 23*, that they *deserve* somebody, something, or a combination of both. It is this *deserving* of someone or something that leads us further down the path of destruction. We make the blessings of life the focus instead of the development of our character, and when we do this, we compromise. I doubt many, if any, people who serve in local church ministry would have ever imagined themselves falling like my new friend did.

When I got into ministry in my early twenties, I was going to change the world for Christ. Now some days, the Americano I drink in the morning is more important to me than my life mission.

It happens. We grow disillusioned with life, and we grow weary of dealing with the brokenness of everyone around us, including ourselves. We battle unforgiveness, bitterness, jealousy, rage, greed, lust, and the list goes on and on. We begin to give in to the voices of entitlement, pleasure seeking, and anything that brings us immediate comfort. We begin to throw off the disciplines of our lives, and we stop allowing correction to be given to us. We see correction as something that only children need, and we refuse to listen to anyone who has an opposing opinion of us. We justify our sin by the good we do, and we start negotiating with God some sort of agreement that allows us to live any way we want privately as long as publicly we do what we told Him we would do.

Over the years this combination of sacrifice, entitlement, disappointment, perpetual brokenness, and ongoing failure leads even the strongest to seek shelter from the truth of their lives.

We want what we can't have, and this creates all kinds of problems in our lives because we are miserable when all we can see is ourselves and what we want. In the book of James, the writer says in chapter 4,

> *What causes quarrels and what causes fights among you? Is it not this, that your passions are at war within you? You desire and do not have, so you murder. You covet and cannot obtain, so you fight and quarrel. You do not have, because you do not*

ask. You ask and do not receive, because you ask wrongly, to spend it on your passions. You adulterous people! Do you not know that friendship with the world is enmity with God? . . . Therefore whoever wishes to be a friend of the world makes himself an enemy of God. Therefore it says, "God opposes the proud, but gives grace to the humble." Submit yourself therefore to God. Resist the devil, and he will flee from you. Draw near to God, and he will draw near to you. Cleanse your hands, you sinners, and purify your hearts, you double-minded. (James 4:1-4, 6-8)

When I am double minded, that means I am saying one thing and living another. This is a very dangerous place to be, especially if you are a spiritual leader who is trying to help other people with the same things. Strangely enough in my own life, I find it easier to justify my own private sin when I am helping others with theirs.

God never takes into consideration how much I am helping others when I refuse to acknowledge my own sin. God would rather show all of us grace, but He can't show grace to someone who refuses to repent and acknowledge their need of it. The wisdom that comes from God is first of all pure, meaning it reflects the character of God. I can't hide my sin and justify it by my good actions for others. This is not the wisdom of God; it is the wisdom of the world. Look at what James says again:

Who is wise and understanding among you? By his good conduct let him show his works in the meekness of wisdom. But if you have bitter jealousy and selfish ambition in your hearts, do not boast and be false to the truth. This is not the wisdom that comes down from above, but is earthly, unspiritual, and demonic. For where jealousy and selfish ambition exist, there will be disorder and every vile practice. But the wisdom from above is first pure, then peaceable, gentle, open to reason, full of mercy, and good fruits, impartial and sincere. (James 3:13-17)

If I hide my sin and justify it by the good I do for others, eventually Numbers 32:23 will be unleashed on me. It is a warning to all of God's people: you can't live any way you want to and justify it by the good you do. God will not overlook your sin because you are helping others with theirs.

Stop thinking God owes you something. Stop chasing primarily after the blessings of God and start seeing the circumstances of your life as God's means for teaching you His wisdom and thus His character for your life.

None of us can avoid sinning forever, but all of us can choose *not* to cover it up. The only time in Scripture I see God getting mad at His people is not when they sin but when they sin and cover it up. What do you need to confess today privately before He makes it known publicly?

"Be sure your sin will find you out" (Numbers 32:23). *The Number 23* ended with the main character being sentenced to prison because his hidden sin that came from his mindset of entitlement was exposed.

Recently I saw a video of Jim Carrey where he was talking to a group of men in a rehabilitation center. He talked to them about suffering leading to salvation. He said, "We have two choices. We can ignore our sin, take the path of self-harm and thus harm others, or we can take the path of grace that Christ provided us through the cross and experience the redemption God has for our lives." I just about wept watching Jim Carrey articulate the gospel, the Good News of Jesus Christ.

I remember when I sat before the presbytery, and they said, "Do you have anything else to say to us?" And I said, "Yes. He has lied no less than five times during this meeting, and this is not a misunderstanding. In time God will expose his sin, and when He does, remember this moment." Those words that came out of my mouth now stand as a warning for my own life—and for yours too. "Be sure your sin will find you out."

I learned through this experience that *life makes sense again with God when He judges and gives consequences to unrepentant, hidden sin in our lives and others'*. We are never to take glory in it when it happens in other people's lives, but this is how God works, and this is how life works again.

The inverse of God's favor and grace is judgment. It doesn't have to end that way for you, me, or others we know. The choice is ours!

Let's be like Jim Carrey: "Let's choose favor and grace." Let's choose the path of suffering that leads to salvation and redemption. And it all begins with confession!

20

JEREMIAH 23:1

J eremiah 23:1-6 says,

> *"Woe to the shepherds [pastors] who destroy and scatter the sheep [God's people] of my pasture!" declares the Lord. Therefore thus says the Lord, the God of Israel, concerning the shepherds who care for my people: "You have scattered my flock and have driven them away, and you have not attended to them. Behold, I will attend to you for your evil deeds, declares the Lord. Then I will gather the remnant of my flock out of all the countries where I have driven them, and I will bring them back to their fold, and they shall be fruitful and multiply. I will set shepherds over them who will care for them, and they shall fear no more, nor be dismayed, neither shall any be missing, declares the Lord. Behold the days are coming, declares the Lord, when I will raise up for David a righteous Branch, and he shall reign as king and deal wisely, and shall execute justice and righteousness in the land. In his days Judah will be saved, and Israel will dwell securely. And this is the name by which he will be called: The Lord is our righteousness.'"*

The shepherds in Jeremiah's day were evil. Their actions destroyed and scattered the people of God. We live in the same kind of situation today.

It seems like every week there is a "big name" pastor or a "little name pastor" who falls because of misuse of church funds, misuse of their sexuality, or an abuse in the use of their power over those they lead that leads to some type of bully pulpit. You don't have to look too far to understand why people are cynical of the church and wary of being led by pastors who make it all about them.

It seems like church vision is more and more perceived as the pastor's selfish ambition wrapped in "God talk" so he can get what he wants out of life through the local church's tithes and offerings. It grieves me as a church planter and as a pastor and more importantly as a shepherd who is supposed to be representing God Almighty. Jeremiah alludes to a "righteous Branch" in Jeremiah 23. This righteous Branch is alluding to what we now know to be Jesus Christ Himself.

In recent past, I had the golden privilege of traveling overseas to the Holy Land for the first time with my college buddy and good friend Joel. We began our trek in the southern Negev where Moses and the people of Israel wandered for forty years in the dessert. It was and is a barren wasteland where literally nothing grows. It is in these sorts of places that it is easy to look up to God and cry out to Him for help. It is in these sorts of surroundings that we are reminded we need God deeply.

However, it is equally easy to then traverse the Holy Land to the northern end and see the land of milk and honey in Tel Dan and surrounding areas. It is easy to see how the people of God could lose sight of their need for God and run wild in their desires and seek to fulfill every ambition their minds could conceive.

As I walked where Jesus walked in the Old City and stood on rocks that He Himself literally walked on two thousand years ago, I couldn't help but be struck by the reality that it is a whole lot easier to walk where Jesus walked than it is to walk like Jesus walked.

Jeremiah 23:1 is not the exception—it is often the rule. It is easy to be a shepherd, a pastor, a spiritual leader, a deacon, a life group leader, an elder, a worship pastor, a Bible teacher, or hold any type of influence over God's people and misuse that power. It is easy to destroy the people of God. It is easy to scatter God's sheep.

Having walked where Jesus walked, I saw shepherds herding sheep. I saw what it may have been like to have walked where Jesus walked, but it didn't help me at all to know how to walk *like* Jesus walked. I didn't meet Jesus while I was in the Holy Land. I didn't run into any of the disciples that Jesus discipled. As a matter a fact, I found the place to be largely pagan, secular, and at times grossly embellished for the sake of gaining a buck or two off tourists who long for an experience.

Don't get me wrong, when I stood at the Mount of Olives I felt emotion that I couldn't have felt by just reading the story. Ever since I went to the Holy Land, when I read the Bible, I don't just see it, I smell it. I highly recommend anyone who can to go visit where Jesus walked, but walking there will remind you, as it did me, that it is a whole lot easier to walk where Jesus walked than to walk like Jesus walked.

My senses regarding personal sin heightened. I found myself tempted to sin in greater ways than ever before. I found myself longing strangely to be a shepherd like Jeremiah described more so than a shepherd like the righteous Branch. How could I be in the Holy Land and not want to be perfect? I was only there for a week and a half.

I was reminded anew in the Holy Land just how broken a man I really am. I was reminded anew just how far I still have to go. I was reminded anew that if I lived during Jeremiah's day, I might have gotten that letter in the mail addressed personally to me and the ministry I lead.

See, sin doesn't take a break just because we want it to, or because we are walking where Jesus walked, or because we just want a break. Sin is ever present and raging in all of us. It is seeking an opportunity to grow at any chance it can get. This is why a short account on sin matters so much. This is why we have to remember that titles given to humans don't make them godly. As a matter a fact, it might make them more susceptible to temptation.

The shepherds in Jeremiah's day hid their sin. Jeremiah was forced to confront their sin by the God he served. As we survey the Old Testament, we learn very quickly that God was long suffering with the His people, but once the leaders for God refused to deal with their own sin, God was left to send prophets to let Israel know its demise was imminent—which is tragic.

If there is one thing Jeremiah's story teaches us, it is this: we can make a difference. We are making a difference, and we can continue to make a difference. Our spiritual leadership matters. However, the effectiveness of our leadership is dictated by how we handle our hidden sin. The greatest gift leaders can give their people, their families, and this world is the gift of being real with the sin in their lives. I have spent over two decades of my life at the same church, and I don't find it easier to be honest about my sin as I age—I find it more difficult. I grow weary of struggling with the same two to three sins every day of my life. I grow weary of having to come back to God over and over again with the same issues.

Sometimes I feel like God looks at me and says, "Not you again." And then when I tell Him what I need to confess to Him, I feel like He says to me, "I am tired of hearing your struggles with sin. I have lost my patience with you growing in these areas." I know theologically this is not true, but practically, come on, doesn't God wear out from hearing the same ol' stuff we struggle with in our lives?

The answer is, no, He doesn't. And by the way, the only other option is to live like the shepherds in Jeremiah 23. I don't want to be that kind of shepherd. I want to be the kind of shepherd spoken of during the birth of the righteous Branch, Jesus Christ. I want to be the kind of shepherd that remains in the field for a lifetime. I know 90 percent of shepherds don't finish in the field. They give up. They quit.

What sin have you stopped paying attention to in your life because you are tired of dealing with it? Through this experience I have learned that *God holds unrepentant leaders accountable, and this is a part of Him teaching us how life makes sense again in His economy.*

Have you thought through how your unconfessed secret sin will end? God is not tired of hearing about your struggle. God is not surprised you can't do this on your own. God sent His righteous Branch because He knew without Him we would all be Jeremiah 23 shepherds.

What brings us out of this? Jeremiah 23:23-24 says, "Am I a God at hand, declares the Lord, and not a God far away? Can a man hide himself in secret places so that I cannot see him? declares the Lord." If you can answer *no* to the latter question, you will be just fine. Don't try to hide from God what you can't. Confess it and forsake it again. You will find that you cannot only walk *where* Jesus walked, but you will also learn to walk *like* Jesus walked.

21

A JOURNEY OF
DOUBLE GRACE

T ake your sin seriously, but once you have, be sure and take God's grace and blessings just as seriously. This is key to pursuing God's voice for a lifetime. When I take my sin more seriously than I take God's grace, I miss hearing God's voice as He applies His grace to my life.

Historically the people of God have seen the voice of God primarily as a tool of judgment and annihilation, not as a tool of grace and blessing. We see this best in Deuteronomy 4:

> *"Did any people ever hear the voice of a god speaking out of the midst of the fire, as you have heard, and still live? Or has any god ever attempted to go and take a nation for himself from the midst of another nation, by trials, by signs, by wonders, and by war, by a mighty hand and an outstretched arm, and by great deeds of terror, all of which the Lord your God did for you in Egypt before your eyes? To you it was shown, that you might know that the Lord is God; there is no other besides him. Out of heaven he let you hear his voice, that he might discipline you. And on earth he let you see his great fire, and you heard his words out*

of the midst of the fire. And because he loved your fathers and chose their offspring after them and brought you out of Egypt with his own presence, by his great power, driving out before you nations greater and mightier than you, to bring you in, to give you their land for an inheritance, as it is this day, know therefore today, and lay it to your heart, that the Lord is God in heaven above and on earth beneath; there is no other." (Deuteronomy 4:33-39, emphasis added)

Hearing God's voice is not a bad thing. You can hear God's voice, live, and be blessed by His grace in your life.

Yes, we must take sin very seriously, but once we have confessed it and received Christ's forgiveness, we must take God's grace just as seriously.

Lest you think this is just an Old Testament thing, Jesus Himself said in John 10:7-11, 16:

So Jesus again said to them, "Truly, truly, I say to you, I am the door of the sheep. All who came before me are thieves and robbers, but the sheep did not listen to them. I am the door. If anyone enters by me, he will be saved and will go in and out and find pasture. The thief comes only to steal and kill and destroy. I came that they may have life and have it abundantly. I [Jesus] am the good shepherd. The good shepherd lays down his life for the sheep. . . . And I [Jesus] have other sheep that are not of this fold. I must bring them also, and they will listen to my voice. So there will be one flock, one shepherd. (emphasis added)

Why is hearing God's voice so important? Because God's voice brings grace and blessing! Everyone can hear the voice of the enemy that brings loss, death, and destruction. Without God's voice we are void of grace and blessing in our lives. It is His voice that brings hope to hopeless situations. It is His voice that brings victory where only defeat has been. It is His voice that tells us what to do with the gifts we have been entrusted with in this life.

It is His voice as we learned in Psalm 23 that leads us beside still waters and makes us to lie down in green pasture. We are reminded again in John 10 that Jesus is that same voice. He is God in the flesh.

He is the Good Shepherd that saves us and leads us to pastures of blessings and grace.

The Bible tells us who God is and what kind of person He wants us to be, but it is His voice that gives us the specifics of our lives that enable us to carry out the unique calling that He has placed on us. There is no substitute for reading God's Word, but there is equally no substitute for listening for the voice of God and responding.

We each have been given a gift, at least one—a gift of grace entrusted to us by God. It is that gift of grace in us that represents the unique purpose God has for our lives. In every situation, we are seeking God's voice to know if we are doing exactly what He has created us to do.

I remember in college before Tosha and I were married, I had a dream that we were married, sitting around the dining room table. We had five kids. In my dream I remembered we had a girl, boy, girl, and twin boys. The details didn't pan out the way I thought they would from the dream, but what did come from that was a willingness of both my wife and I to struggle through over one and a half years of trying to overcome physical illnesses so we could get pregnant with our fifth child. I had given up on hearing God. Tosha could still hear God's voice, and she believed we were *still* to have a fifth child. I came up with *all* the reasons why it wasn't working. She asked us to keep trying. We did.

On May 2, 2006, Annaka Journey Grace Williams was born. Her name means *grace upon grace* or a *journey of double grace*. Her name comes from the combination of a worship song our worship pastor at the time, Richie Fike, wrote, called "Worshipper." The line goes like this: "I am a worshipper journeying onward in spite of all I have lost." The rest of her name comes from John 1:16: "For from his [Jesus'] fullness we have all received, grace upon grace." There it is, a journey of double grace. Annaka means *grace*. When we *listen* for God's voice, we don't just get a journey full of grace—we get a double journey of grace. God wants us to experience and obey His voice more than anything else in our lives.

In 1 Samuel 15:22-23, Samuel said, "'Has the Lord as great a delight in burnt offerings and sacrifices, as in obeying the voice of the Lord? Behold, to obey [His voice] is better than sacrifice, and to listen [to His voice] than the fat of rams. For rebellion [not listening to and obeying God's voice] is as the sin of divination [witchcraft], and presumption is as iniquity and idolatry." God takes us listening for and obeying His voice very seriously. Repentance still matters to God—just as it did back then.

Now I know there are scores of believers who say, "We have God's Word; we don't need dreams and visions to know what God wants today." Acts 2:17 says, "And in the *last* days [—they haven't occurred yet] it shall be, God declares, that I will pour out my Spirit on *all* flesh, and your sons and your daughters shall prophesy, and your young men shall see visions, and your old men shall dream dreams" (emphasis added). God wants us to be disciplined to hear from Him through His Word, but that is *not* the only source by which God speaks. He also speaks to us through the Holy Spirit that lives inside us through various means—including visions and dreams.

There are many examples of very godly people who had God's Word but relied as well on hearing God's voice in dreams and visions, angles, stars, dice, drawing straws, even donkeys—and the list goes on and on and on. I know this is dangerous territory for someone who believes in the inerrancy of Scripture like I do, but nonetheless, it is still very real and very legitimate.

How did Balaam know what to do when Barak wanted him to curse Israel in the Old Testament? A donkey talked to him on behalf of God and told him not to do it. How did Joseph know what to do with Mary when she turned up pregnant before they got married? God came to him in a dream and told him this was of Him. Instead of putting Mary and the future Son of God away, he obeyed the voice of God in the dream and kept her safe until she gave birth and didn't consummate their marriage until after this.

How did Joseph know that Herod wanted baby Jesus dead? God revealed it to him by an angel in a dream and thus he fled to Egypt to keep Jesus safe. How did the disciples decide who to pick to replace Judas? They drew straws, in essence. How did Paul know where to go on his next missionary journey in Acts 16? "And a vision appeared to Paul in the night: a man of Macedonia was standing there, urging him and saying, 'Come over to Macedonia and help us.' And when Paul had seen the vision, *immediately* we sought to *go* into

Macedonia, *concluding* that God had called us to preach the gospel to them" (Acts 16:9-10, emphasis added). The Apostle Paul wrote half the New Testament for God. He relied on visions and dreams to know the specific will of God for his life.

And I think the final trump card for listening for God's voice is John 10:16: "They [my sheep] will listen to my voice." It doesn't say listen *for*, it says listen *to* my voice. God's voice is *not* a random occurrence. It is a consistent occurrence. Yes, He uses His written Word to convey the whole counsel of truth, but He uses the Holy Spirit inside of us to teach us specifically how we are to live and what we are to do with our lives. I don't believe we have the freedom to do whatever we want. I don't believe I can pastor anywhere and be in God's will. I don't believe I can be married to anyone and be in God's will. I don't believe I can teach whatever I want from Scripture whenever I want and be in God's will.

Let me prove it to you in Acts 16:6-7: "And they [Paul and his team] went through the region of Phrygia and Galatia, having been forbidden by the Holy Spirit to speak the word in Asia. And when they had come up to Mysia, they attempted to go into Bithynia, but the Spirit of Jesus did not allow them." What? God didn't let them share Him, and He didn't allow them to go to Bithynia. How did God reveal this? It doesn't say; it must have been circumstances or a feeling or a conversation or maybe a dream or vision. Regardless, even within God's permissive will, He has a specific plan for your life. It is unique to you and cannot be duplicated by others.

He wants me to *ask*, *listen*, and *do* exactly what He tells me to do with my life every day. No, I am not a robot. And no, I don't always get it right, as you have seen in this story of our fifth born— where we thought through a series of fleeces we were to stop having children, but then we had a divine moment that changed the outcome, and we got pregnant with our fifth child. But like I say, I don't believe that when I get to heaven, God will say I tried too hard to ask, listen, and do what His voice told me specifically to do.

Remember, this journey is a journey of double grace. He rewards those who sincerely seek Him, not those who always get it right. However, that does not mean we do not need to learn how to *hear* God and in turn *do* what He tells us to do. God is a rewarder of those who sincerely seek Him. It is better to obey God's voice than to make the greatest spectacle of sacrifice anyone has ever seen.

When you get to heaven, God will not judge you on what He told somebody else to do with their life. He will judge you based on what He told you to do with your life. Therefore, stop comparing your life to someone else's. What God has told you to do is unique to you.

Are you sincerely seeking Him? Then rest in the fact that this is a journey of double grace! He wants you to know that you can't screw your life up if you are committed to repentance.

Through the experience with the fleece and our fifth child, I have learned that *life makes sense again when God applies grace upon grace to the repentant*. Repentance still matters to God. Join me in it and listen.

As young Samuel said, "Speak, your servant is listening" (1 Samuel 3:10 NLT).

That's all God asks.

THE HAUNT OF HOPE IN 23

W hen I first started seeing *23*s, it was all for seemingly negative outcomes. I have lost hours, days, weeks, and even months, maybe even years of my life trying to understand why God would use such a strange way to reveal to me what He wanted me to do with my life in a specific situation. But I have learned over the years that God uses physical circumstances to get our spiritual attention.

What used to be a completely negative symbol and reminder, God has taken and redeemed over the years. Truly, *23* has become my Romans 8:28: "And we know that for those who love God all things work together for good, for those who are called according to his purpose." What used to be a torture has now become a reminder of God's favor, grace, and love over my life.

After the ordeal with my new friend, I continued to see *23* randomly over and over and over again in my life. It angered me. Every time I saw it, it forced my heart to think about all the unanswered questions of this situation. It forced me to wrestle with the tension I felt toward God because He asked me to do something that seemingly turned out the way it would have had I done *nothing*.

I had scores of leaders, pastors, and close friends and family tell me that they wouldn't have been able to do what I did. They didn't mean it this way, but I heard, *You're a BIG idiot!* I felt like a fool.

Why God? Why did You ask me to do something that turned out the way it would have had I done nothing? His response seemed to be silence with more and more examples of *23*.

Then it happened. After positive things occurred in my life, I would see the number *23* randomly in situations. The number started to be associated with something in my life besides this very negative and seemingly unredeemed situation in my life.

I had a pastor friend on the East Coast that started getting prophetic words for me, and he had never gotten prophetic words in his entire life. He felt so strongly that God was prompting him to share these messages that he would text them to me. They would be spot on, and often they would come to me with a time that had a *23* in it, like 1:23 or 2:23 or 3:23.

It was spooky all over again, except this time it felt redemptive. When I saw the number, I was starting to feel hope from it instead of despair. When I saw the number, I was starting to remember good situations instead of the impending and overhanging sorrowful situation regarding "the man."

The week after my new friend fell, our church took in $23,000.00 in our regular weekly tithes and offerings. Since then I have had so many positive financial situations that had "23s" in them that I have lost count.

Now my own wife, who has lived through all of this with me and believes in me more than anyone else in my life, often chides me about this "23," and I often still feel crazy about it and should put it aside for a *more reasonable and rational* explanation that good evangelicals can accept, process, and duplicate—but I can't. Thankfully my second born, Christianna, continues to work on Tosha to make her a believer.

I know this is going to sound crazy to think and even more crazy to say: God has used the number *23* to change my life. Now, when I am down, discouraged, wanting to quit, need a reminder of God's grace and hope in my life, inevitably the number *23* appears.

One time when I was discouraged and needed a reminder that God was in this *23* stuff, one of the guys in my life group, Joel, started waking up often at 2:23 a.m. It happens so much now that he has stopped mentioning it to me. This was a small encouragement and reminder through someone close to me that God was still present.

As I stated previously, a few years ago I had the privilege of going to Israel for the first time in my life with my roommate from college, Joel. While there, I looked up one of my church friends who served in the military in Special Operations. At the time, he was leading counter terrorism efforts. Needless to say, I felt quite safe with him as we walked through the Old City.

As he and I journeyed down the Via Dolorosa, we discussed things like stigmata, dreams and visions of old saints, and various mystical experiences we had each had (mysticism being used here in the sense of spiritual intuition of truths believed to transcend ordinary understanding). If you have been to the Old City, you know such a journey brings out the mysticism in the most unmystical person alive.

I started sharing with him about this *23* thing and how God spoke to me about "the man" through it—how God used it to give me corresponding Scripture to confirm what He was revealing to me about him. At one point in the journey to the cross in the Old City, I could tell he was obliging me, and even though he prided himself on being a mystic, I was weirding him out.

We stopped and faced one another on the Via Dolorosa (the road of suffering for Christ to the Cross—*stations of the cross*). At some point, as I described this "*23*," he motioned to me to turn. When I turned over my left shoulder, on the wall was carved "*23*." Not only that, but the second number was "44." I get cold chills writing this. I felt the Holy Spirit come over me and consume me. The number 44 is my wife's favorite number and has always been, for her, the number that gave her a sense of hope or happiness when she thought of it. This, for me, was a double confirmation through randomly ordered events.

Here this tough operative dude later told me that he was weirded out by my story, but when we stopped, and he looked over my shoulder and saw the number on the wall, it really freaked him out. See, it has happened to me so many times now that I no longer doubt it or question it or wonder about it. I know some of the stories from Jeff's life and from his military career. He has lived a pretty bizarre story himself. And if it weirds a dude like him out, I get it. I must be a real head case.

Nevertheless, I see it as God's sign to me that He sees me, knows me, appreciates what I did for Him, and is going to shower me with grace and blessings because of my obedience to His voice.

Sometimes I become a doubting Thomas myself and get jaded about what I have experienced because it is so weird and hard to explain to others. Sometimes I try to talk myself out of it, and when I do, I hear all kinds of voices in my head that agree with me and tell me things like, *Who do you think you are that God would care about you that much?* And then I say, *Yeah, that's right, I'm an idiot. Who in their right mind would believe this stuff? I'm a nobody, and God wouldn't take the time to be this gracious and kind to me.* However, every time I go down this rabbit hole, my heavenly Father sends yet another reminder to me that though I may be a kook, it is not because of this.

I have learned through this experience that *life with God begins to make sense again when we see the physical symbols that once reminded us of discouraging things now bringing reminders of redemption to our lives.*

Just a few years ago, on our Christmas holiday, our family went on a drive to look at lights and drive through a beautiful historic area. We all piled into the truck and looked at the clock for some reason—it was 5:23 p.m. We looked at it and laughed. I even thought, *coincidence.* We went to get ice cream, and when we came out to get back in the truck, we turned it on and one of the kids said, "Look, Dad! It's 6:23 p.m." We all laughed again. On our way back, we stopped off for a little coffee. When we got back in the truck, Tosha noticed: 7:23 p.m. She laughed aloud. I said, "God, we get it. Thank You for Your favor."

I believe because of the past thirteen years of experiencing this number that God uses physical things to get our spiritual attention. I have seen this now over and over again in my life. What started out as a terrible nightmare has now turned into a haunt of hope. Do you know what the meaning of the word *haunt* is when used as a noun? One of the meanings is, *a meeting place.* See, *23* has become a meeting place of hope.

It used to haunt me in a negative sense—but not anymore. No pain in our lives is lost in God's economy of redemption. No pain is wasted. No pain. Ask God to turn the symbols of your pain from feelings of discouragement to feelings of redemption.

When I turn the corner in my kitchen and head toward the bedroom—the bedroom clock says 6:23 p.m. The heavy burdens of that day of ministry just fly off my shoulders. When I wake up in the middle of the night in a hot sweat from doing spiritual warfare prayers in my sleep and look over at the clock—it says 1:23 a.m. The weight of the darkness lifts, and I hear the Lord say, "I am here with you, and I am well pleased with you."

When I drive to church to preach a message in our many weekly weekend services, I feel the weight of ministering, praying, and wrestling through the pain of people's lives. I look down at my truck clock and I see 8:23 a.m., and the burden turns into a blessing. I hear the Lord say, "I picked you to do this. I believe in you. You can do this."

When I drive to a meeting late at night or early in the morning, in the dark, and I wrestle through the aloneness I feel, I look down at the clock, and I hear the Lord say, "You are not alone, I am with you."

See, *23* is no longer a symbol. When I see it, it is God's voice. It is God speaking to me immediately. We all need this. We all need a *haunt of hope*, a meeting place of hope. Where is your meeting place of hope? Where do you turn to get refocused and feel God's presence, favor, and pleasure again? How do you know you are doing what God the Father has asked you to do?

I am no longer ashamed of *23* and the phenomenon it has become in my life. I accept the kookiness of it. God has used it to lift the shame of my new friend off my life, and He has refocused my attention through it to live each and every boring, who cares day of my life looking for His voice.

I am not special or unique. He wants to do the same for you. He wants to create for you a haunt of hope, a meeting place of hope.

Will you meet Him there today?

What's Your "23"?

My friend Seth has walked with me through a lot of the quirkiness of *23*. Recently he said to me, "Kelly, I think the point of this book is *not* the number *23* but that everyone has a *23* and that God uses it to reveal His favor, grace, and love to them—especially when they are going through a hard time—so that they can hear and discern God's voice and direction for their life."

My friend is pretty smart! Don't tell him I said that.

The question of this book is, What's your *23*? What symbol, number, memory, reoccurring motif does God use to remind you that He has not forgotten about you and He still sees what is going on in your life? What does He use to speak to you when nothing else seems to get through the dark cloud that surrounds your head and heart?

The most important lesson I have learned through this crazy *23* process is this: *God gives us reoccurring physical reminders that He is FOR us.* And that is *all* that matters, especially in the end.

Eric Liddle, the great Olympian runner in the 1930s, used to say, "When I run, I feel the pleasure of God on my life." Running, for him, was his "23." My good friend Jon Elsberry feels the pleasure of God the most when he is praying, and is he a prayer warrior! That man can pray forever! I have learned to stand during our weekly prayer times together, otherwise I find myself in the posture the disciples found themselves in when Jesus asked them to tarry one hour with Him in the Garden of Gethsemane—asleep. Sorry, Jon!

We all have something that when we do it, see it, experience it, or relive it, it reminds us of God's faithful voice whispering, speaking, and sometimes even shouting His grace and love into our lives. Like me, it may be a symbol God has taken and turned from a negative to a positive. But all of us have something.

When I gave this talk about my *23* experiences at the church I pastor, a number of people said they had seasons in their life where they saw their favorite number in the most random and unexpected times. There were other people who spoke of reoccurring dreams, visions, and even life experiences that occurred to them over and over again, and each time it gave them a deep sense of God's closeness in their lives and the courage to hear God's voice again.

In this final chapter, I want you to ask yourself the question, maybe for the first time in your life, *What is my "23"?* What reoccurring symbol, theme, or experience does God use in your life to remind you of His favor, presence, and love, so that you can discern His voice and direction for your life?

As I have shared this bizarre story with people, I get more positive than negative feedback. Oh, I'm used to the weird looks and the awkward stares and laughs. Like King David said to Michael when he saw him dancing before the Lord and told him to stop, he responded, "I will become more undignified in the presence of my Lord." My thoughts exactly! I don't want to become more dignified in my faith as I grow older if that means I become more jaded.

However, I am thankful I have degrees from Liberty University and Dallas Theological Seminary hanging on my wall, and my wife and I have planted a thriving Southern Baptist church that is taking steps as I write this to launch its third location. I'm not a kook. Well, I may be a kook but not because of this.

I no longer need or even want to "make sense" of everything in my life. I am not even sure sometimes why I see the number or what the point is; I just love the reassuring feeling that comes from experiencing it every time. I sense, in my spirit, the Lord say, *I am here. I see what you did for Me and it matters, and I will bless you for it.* Yes, it is weird, but it is a part of me now, and I believe I will carry this with me for the rest of my life.

The strangeness of the numbers and the prophetic experience with my new friend is the surroundings and circumstances God used to teach me of His voice, will, love, and favor for my life. I feel a deep sense of connectedness to God, and when I wake up in the night, I just assume God wants to say something to me. When I see the number, I assume God is speaking to me even though I might not know at the time what He is saying.

Just last week, I took my wife out on a date. We passed a car dealership, and both of us simultaneous looked out the window where their large digital clock was flashing "6:23 p.m." We both immediately looked down at the clock in our truck, and it said "5:19 p.m." I looked at Tosha and said, "What is that all about?" She laughed and said, "I don't know, but at some point you just have to believe."

What are you refusing to believe and see? It is easy to be a skeptic, and the older we get the more likely we are to become negative, bitter, jaded, and sarcastic—to convince ourselves that God may love us, but He is not too concerned about the intimate details of our lives. I know, especially if you are overly skeptical, you may say, "I don't have anything like that in my life. God never speaks to me."

Listen, if you are God's child, He has and is speaking to you. Now don't go further down the rabbit hole and conclude, "Well then I must not be a Christian." You are a Christian if you have put your faith and trust in Jesus Christ as your Lord and Savior. That is settled. What isn't settled is all the voices in your life that try to drown out the still small voice of God who wants to connect to you not just sometimes but *all* the time.

He doesn't just want to be intimate with the "important" or "special" celebrity Christians in the body of Christ. He wants to be intimate with *all* His children—and He is. He loves you and He is speaking to you through His Word, through nature, through recurring themes, through relationships, through dreams, through visions, and yes, maybe even through a crazy thing like the number *23*. Certainly there is nothing magical or mysterious about the number; it is the one God picked for me, and He uses anything and everything to give to us this continual reminder. We matter to Him more than anything else in this world. It is time to lay down the defenses and let God engulf you with His voice.

And do you know why this is important? Because without His voice in your life, you can't feel His presence—that is what His voice is, it is His presence. It is the most important thing about a real relationship with Jesus Christ.

God told the nation of Israel, "And these words that I command you today shall be on your heart. You shall teach them diligently to your children, and shall talk of them when you sit in your house, and when you walk by the way, and when you lie down, and when you rise. You shall bind them as a sign on your hand, and they shall be as frontlets between your eyes. You shall write them on the doorposts of your house and on your gates" (Deuteronomy 6:6-9).

I have watched so many people go through church pain and be hurt by a celebrity pastor and experience things like I did that leave you feeling disillusioned by the church. Fight it! It is the enemy. He wants you to stop believing God speaks and that He can be intimate with you for a lifetime. He wants you to grow bitter and jaded by the politics of the church. Don't get me wrong, I love the local church, but I see the same things everyone else sees and watched for years, wondering if God saw, and if He did, did He care?

Every one of us is in a spiritual battle to give up and give in to the lethargy of the day. Our nation is in a battle to give into the lethargy of the day. Every person committed to the local church is in a battle to give into the lethargy of the day. If we don't beat it, we will join them. What are we going to do to combat that?

For Eric Liddle, when he ran, he remembered God's favor and pleasure in His life. If you travel today to Ground Zero you will see what is now called the Freedom Tower, which is a monument erected to remind us of the sacrifices made by so many that day— not just the ones who lost their lives in the crash but those who gave of themselves to save the lives of their fellow human beings. I have never been more proud of our nation than I was that day.

This monument stands high in the air to fight against the lethargy of the day as a reminder of the heroism of so many people on that dreadful day who used their presence, their voices, and their very lives for us to rescue, love, and save people in the midst of the chaos, debris, and shear hatred of the enemies that launched that attack on the US—as Jesus used and continues to use His life, death and resurrection for the salvation of His people. Since 9/11 our nation has changed, but Osama bin Laden did not win, Al Qaeda did not win, and we have not given up. Our nation has stood and will continue to stand against the tyranny of the day.

Just like the Freedom Tower stands as a reminder of our nation's faithfulness to each other and the freedom for our world, so when I see the number *23*, it immediately reminds me of how God has taken the pain of a very dark and sad situation and turned it into something good. I feel God when I see it. I feel God's pleasure for me when I see it. I hear God's voice through it among a variety of other things in my life as well, like His Word. It helps me fight against the lethargy of my own soul and that which is all around me.

What reminds you of God's pleasure and favor for your life? What gives you the hope you need to hear God's voice speak to you during the dark moments and seasons of your life and fight for what matters?

I want to invite you right now to kneel tonight—alone, with your spouse, or with a trusted friend—and pray this prayer:

Dear Heavenly Father,

I believe You are real. I believe Your voice is real. I want to hear Your voice in my routine, everyday, who cares kind of life. I ask You, in Jesus' name, to give me a reoccurring theme that I can see that will remind me of Your favor and pleasure for me and give me the hope that You are speaking into my life so I can discern Your voice and continue to battle and do what You have called me to do for a lifetime, for Your glory, Jesus.

Speak, Lord Jesus. Your servant is listening.

Sincerely,

Your favored child

AUTHOR'S AFTERWORD
QUESTIONS AND ANSWERS

Publisher's Note: Before publication, an advance review copy of this book was made available to several trusted theologians and pastors. We asked them for their opinions about whether this story, presented as a true story, violated any essential biblical truths or Christian orthodoxy (using the Nicene Creed as the foundation for assessment of the latter). No direct concerns were raised regarding alignment with either biblical truths or Christian orthodoxy; however, a number of requests were made for clarifications and generally for more insights into a variety of "likely" topics on which many readers may seek more detail. The author then addressed each of these questions, which are presented below in a Q&A format. Similar questions were grouped together for ease of response and review.

1. **QUESTION: What were your motives for sharing your story with the public?**

   ANSWER: Ultimately, I want to encourage others who, like me, have done what God asked them to do and yet find that their lives have been turned upside down. Perhaps the situation has hurt them or shamed them, like me. I want all who travel this difficult path to know that in the end, God still sees them. God is still for them, and He will bless them for what they have done for Him.

   I hope that by sharing my story, I can encourage others to keep chasing hard after God and pursuing whatever God has asked them to do regardless of the results. I hope that sharing my story will help rekindle people's naïve obedience to follow God's leading regardless of the outcome, simply trusting God that our flawed faithfulness is enough. I hope that by sharing my story, more believers will faithfully use the gifts God has granted them and administer them fully for His kingdom during their lifetime. I hope that by sharing my story, many will see that, like Elijah, they are not alone. God has others just like them who have said, "I will serve my God faithfully in my generation."

I also want every reader to understand that sharing my story was not an easy decision, nor one I made lightly. Sharing such a personal story is uncomfortable and difficult at best, and sharing it transparently, as I've sought to do, is doubly so. Does any pastor really want to share that the doubts, wounds, and fears they've experienced almost drove them out of the ministry—almost caused them to abandon their faith? It took years for me to find the courage to write about these events. I had to work my way through many things: Did God really want me to share this painful season of my life? What would people think? What of my reputation? How would my family, the church I pastor, and the community be impacted? In the end, I simply felt compelled to share my story. I believe I'm called to do so.

2. **QUESTION: How did you confirm that your vision was actually from God? How did you move from the point of having a vision to deciding to actually take action to go talk to "the man" about such a difficult topic? Did you adhere to any accountability process/people? What Scripture anchored or informed your decisions along the way? How long did it take from the time you received the vision until you had the final meeting with "the man"?**

ANSWER: The steps I share below occurred over a seven-month period of time. I list them as "steps" simply for ease of communicating. At the time, I didn't think of them that way. I didn't layout a specific process to follow. I was just seeking to determine God's will, and as a believer I turned to God in prayer and His Word, and to family and trusted friends and counselors to help affirm my path.

Step 1: I received a vision in the night from God. I was startled out of a deep sleep. I sat up in bed. I looked at the clock and it read *1:23* in bold red letters. I looked straight ahead, and I started to see visual images of a man who was doing things he shouldn't have been doing. I felt the feelings (I assume) God felt toward the actions of this man. At first, I couldn't see who the man was, but in my spirit, I somehow knew. I would describe this experience loosely the way Ezekiel describes his vision in the beginning of his book. That is, I saw something above me, and I felt the emotional effect toward the man's (sinful) actions. I could see images and feel impressions. It was like nothing else I've experienced, but to put it in terms others might relate to, it was something akin to watching a movie while experiencing a visceral, gut feeling/intuition-type impression of the implications.

Step 2: I tested that vision against Scripture (e.g., *Is there anything about this vision that contradicts Scripture?* If so, it couldn't be from God as He never contradicts Himself. *Could I find an example in the Bible of this thing happening to another one of God's children?* If yes, that would tend to affirm. See more about affirming Scripture below). I didn't find anything about my experience that contradicted Scripture or scriptural principles, and there were many examples of God speaking to His people. So I continued to pray and ask God to help me understand.

Step 3: This initial vision and experience was confusing to me. But it began to reoccur often (as I describe in the book), and over time, the Spirit inside of me told me what I was seeing, who it was, and most importantly, what I was to do. For example, I would see impressions and then I would hear in my spirit, "I am not pleased with what this person is doing. He is . . ." The voice became more specific as time went on, and eventually the voice told me who the man was. My confidence that God was actually revealing this to me grew with repetition, as did my clarity and understanding. When I would go to Scripture I would read of characters in the Bible like Saul, and God would say, "This man is acting like that man." I believe God was confirming through His Scripture and these experiences that what I was seeing in the visions was from Him. They kept recurring—and I did not act on any part of this vision until it had been repeatedly confirmed through God's Word and the Spirit. I believe visions, dreams, and words that are from God will never contradict or supersede the already revealed Word of God in the Bible. The Bible is the foundation and the boundary for all words that God will give today. So as the pattern kept recurring, I started writing it down in my journal to create a written record and also for accountability.

Step 4: I shared what was happening with my wife and three close friends to get objectivity.

Step 5: I eventually realized it was not going to go away. Because I am in a public position of authority, accountable to a local church, I decided to go to my elders and submit this experience to them for accountability, feedback, and discernment.

With each of the remaining steps, I consulted my elders, spouse, and a few trusted friends from here on out to make sure I was being accountable and attempting to glean their wisdom and perspective on the things I was experiencing.

Step 6: I went to a service at "the man's" church to see if I would receive confirmation in my spirit, while in his presence, listening to him preach. During the service, I kept hearing in my mind a phrase similar to Matthew 8:15: "His vision is for me but his heart is far from me." I took this to mean that the vision I was having had merit.

Step 7: I contacted him to see if we could get together for coffee or lunch so I could get to know him in a social setting to further test the words and visions I was receiving. The lunch took a while to happen, but eventually the meeting confirmed in various ways that what I was sensing had merit. I shared these findings with my accountability team.

Step 8: During this time, visions, dreams, words from God, Scripture, and "coincidental events," like being awakened in the night at 1:23 a.m., then 2:31 a.m., then 3:21 a.m. became a consistent pattern in my life. I began to see these events and times as a sign. I would hear in my head, *Read Psalm 23:1*—and so on. I began to assume after many occurrences that the time God awoke me had something to do with a corresponding Scripture reference (which I talk about more fully in the book). Eventually I stopped assuming all this was "random" and started to see the patterns. I began to believe God was affirming His vision to me through these events.

Step 9: At times, the weight of the vision would get excessively heavy. That is, I would feel a strong leading to take another step toward talking with "the man." At these times, I used Gideon's interaction with God as an example. I asked God to affirm this leading was from him—like Gideon had done with the fleece. I would pray something like, "Lord, if You want me to contact him, then let my devotion for that day be about someone confronting someone else in sin." These "fleeces" would randomly pop in my head, and I would then pray them. When they came true, I would take that to mean the leading was from God and that I was to take the next step that was before me.

Step 10: After several months, and after receiving many confirmations that my vision and leading were from God, I came to the point of realizing that I needed to be obedient and follow God's promptings to meet with "the man." I had documented these findings in my journals, and I knew I had to go in humility and love or not at all. I called my accountability team and said, "I need to contact 'the man' and share this vision with him, recognizing that I could be wrong." They blessed my decision, and I went forth and engaged the spiritual findings on a physical level.

Step 11: I set up a meeting. We met. I shared my journal entries about my vision and what God was leading me to do. I still had no idea, humanly, whether my vision was true. I asked him to please show mercy on me if I was wrong. Instead, he confirmed verbally to me that what I had been shown in the vision about his sin was true.

Step 12: I asked him to share this same confirmation with his spiritual authority. He told me that he would. However, he called a week later with a very different message. He berated me and said he would not confirm any wrongdoing with his accountability team. In response, I asked who his spiritual authority was so that I could discharge this information to them. He gave me his worship pastor's contact information. I asked him to confirm that his worship pastor was his spiritual authority. I doubted that his worship pastor could be his spiritual authority but accepted the information. I told him that if he would not share this information with his spiritual authority after a certain time, then I would (but only to his spiritual authority).

Step 13: A few days later, the head of "the man's" presbytery called me. He said that they were setting up a meeting to discuss the situation. He asked me to attend. I brought two elders, and the head of the presbytery brought his elder board and "the man's" wife. The meeting occurred in a conference room at a hotel. The atmosphere was like a courtroom. In the end, the presbytery chose "the man's" word over mine. They instead accused me of making unsubstantiated accusations. I was devastated. I agreed in this meeting not to speak of the situation publicly or to share it with anyone outside of those who had been involved in this meeting.

Step 14: I said nothing publicly for five years, while "the man" sought to discredit me and destroy the ministry the Lord had called me to lead. During this time his wife sent me a five-page, handwritten, signed letter addressing various aspects of the presbytery meeting. I still have a copy of that letter. During this season I struggled mightily with hurt, anger, and feelings of, *Why God?* This was the longest five years of my life. But I clung to the example of King David during the time of Saul and refused to touch God's anointed (i.e., I never responded to the attacks made against me by "the man," even though I didn't understand what God's plan was during this time or why He would allow this to happen).

Step 15: When the news about "the man's" private life broke publicly, I wept for days. I couldn't believe it was finally over. The hidden ways of "the man" were exposed publicly in the papers and television. I was relieved, but the wounds were deep and the brokenness was great in me. I contacted "the man," but he refused to talk with me and abruptly hung up the phone from our conversation.

Step 16: I was never contacted by the presbytery. I contacted the leader once. We had a brief interchange in person at a conference at which he was speaking.

Step 17: About four or five years ago, I was reading Brené Brown's books on shame and realized the shame of this had my heart stuck, and I needed healing. As I read one of her books, I felt a prompting to put down on paper this experience.

Step 18: I sat at a Starbucks off and on for weeks, penning this experience and combing back through my journals. It brought a measure of peace to me and started the healing process inside of me.

Step 19: I began to wonder if others needed the same kind of healing as me.

Step 20: I contacted the pastor and asked him if he would join me in writing a book that talked about the experience and see if he and I could experience some mutual healing, redemption, and restoration. He refused. He, to this day, doesn't see me as a "player" in his life and refuses to acknowledge to me the role I played in his life.

Step 21: I put out a series of fleeces because I knew this book should not be published if I was the only one who thought so.

Step 22: I prepared the manuscript for publishing.

Step 23: I pray you experience the healing I have experienced through making this public, and I pray that redemption can come someday to the one I had to confront. It is my prayer that you find your *23*, your reoccurring physical reminder that enables you to know God sees, He hears, He cares, and He is still for you regardless of the outcome.

3. **QUESTION: How does the process you followed align with Scripture? More specifically, what does Scripture say about addressing another believer's sin? And how do you strike a balance between obedience—doing what you believe God has asked you to do about another person's sin—and wisdom—being submissive and accountable to others along the way?**

ANSWER:

> *Brothers, if anyone is caught in any transgression, you who are spiritual should restore him in a spirit of gentleness. Keep watch on yourself, lest you too be tempted. Bear one another's burdens, and so fulfill the law of Christ. For if anyone thinks he is something, when he is nothing, he deceives himself. But let each one test his own work, and then his reason to boast will be in himself alone and not in his neighbor. For each will have to bear his own load. Let the one who is taught the word share all good things with the one who teaches. Do not be deceived: God is not mocked, for whatever one sows, that will he also reap. For the one who sows to his own flesh will from the flesh reap corruption, but the one who sows to the Spirit will from the Spirit reap eternal life. And let us not grow weary of doing good, for in due season we will reap, if we do not give up. So then, as we have opportunity, let us do*

good to everyone, and especially to those who are of the household of faith. (Galatians 6:1-10)

Here is what I believe this passage teaches and what the principles are that Paul is teaching us from his confrontation with Peter in Galatians 2. As followers of Jesus, we have a responsibility to hold one another accountable. Paul was not in charge of Peter. In general terms, we are to follow levels of leadership and accountability. Most of the time this will occur through systems set in place, but when those systems are not functioning correctly or effectively, God will use other means to hold someone accountable and may even bring in a "special counsel or vision or dream" to try and get the accountability process to work again or be affective. But regardless of the construct, here are the principles that dictate how we should go about confronting another believer in Jesus that has unconfessed sin in his or her life:

i.   Restore the person in a "spirit of gentleness."

ii. Bear others' burdens for them—not just the ones you want to bear or think you are entitled to bear. There is ultimately only one church: Jesus' church.

iii. Keep watch on yourself that you don't fall into the same temptation because of pride.

iv. Don't deceive yourself that you are above sin while you are trying to help someone else with theirs.

v.   Warn the person with love.

vi. Don't grow weary in doing good regardless of the outcome. Don't give up. (This is the hardest part for me.)

vii.   Do good to everyone, especially those in the house of faith. You have to see this as you trying to help someone be restored. If you can't, you shouldn't do it. God corrects in order to redeem—not destroy.

Regardless of what we do for God, we must be accountable and submitted to authority.

> *Let every person be subject to the governing authorities. For there is no authority except from God, and those that exist have been instituted by God. (Romans 13:1)*

Test the spirits as described in the twenty-three-step process above.

> *Do not despise prophecies, but test everything; hold fast what is good. (1 Thessalonians 5:20-21)*

Act in obedience to what God has asked you to do regardless of the outcome in the context of accountability.

> *Therefore I endure everything for the sake of the elect, that they also may obtain the salvation that is in Christ Jesus with eternal glory. (1 Timothy 2:10)*

4. QUESTION: Why do you compare 9/11 to this experience?

ANSWER: Because of the coincidental timing of my story and the horrific attack of 9/11, the two events will forever be linked in my mind. However, by no means am I trying to imply that the pain I went through in any way matches the pain, suffering, and loss countless people endured during the 9/11 tragedy. The analogy serves only to give perspective on the depths of the spiritual battle that was waged at this time in my heart.

5. QUESTION: Does everyone have a *23* experience?

ANSWER:

> *For what can be known about God is plain to them, because God has shown it to them. For his invisible attributes, namely, his eternal power and divine nature, have been clearly perceived, ever since the creation of the world, in the things that have been made. (Romans 1:19-20)*

Since the beginning of time, God has used physical things to reveal His eternal and spiritual glory. Romans 1:19-20 tell us that what God created proves God exists, and if we look to the physical things He created we can know a spiritual and eternal God exists.

The number *23* is a physical representation of God's spiritual presence in my life. It started off as a negative thing, but God, as described in the book, eventually redeemed it and turned it into a redemptive positive. I believe that God has a physical reminder for everyone that He is present in the world. It may be as expansive as the creation of the world, or it may be as specific as something like the number *23*. I believe if you look back over your life of faith, you will see reoccurring physical reminders of God's presence. I believe it is OK to look for these *23*s and allow them to give you hope again that God sees, hears, and is still for you. I challenge the reader to look for these physical patterns of repetition in their own story and see them as from God.

6. **QUESTION: What do you think is the main message of your story? Do you see it as a call to repentance? Is the main message that God goes to extraordinary lengths to try to recover a lost sheep? Is it that you reap what you sow? Is it that God still talks to us through visions and dreams? Is the main point that we should listen to God's voice and do whatever He asks? If the reader misses everything else, what is the one thing you want them to act on after reading this book?**
   ANSWER:

   i. *What do you think is the main message of your story?* I believe the main message of The Mystery of 23: God Speaks is just that: God speaks to us still today, and He uses a physical means like the number 23 to remind us of a spiritual truth that He sees us, He is with us, and most importantly, He is for us. I would invite the reader to look for reoccurring spiritual truths in the physical realm of their life. For me it is 23, for Eric Liddle it was running. All of us have something physical in our lives that when we experience the repetition of it, we feel close to God or feel God's pleasure for us. Every person I have discussed this book with tells me of a physical means that reminds them of God's presence in their lives. I haven't talked to anyone yet that can't tell me what their physical means is that reminds them of God's spiritual presence and favor for and in their lives. To me this is the point of the book: to restore their confidence in God's presence and voice in their life through repetitious, physical means.

ii. *Do you see it as a call to repentance?* I believe this is a secondary effect of the book, but yes. I believe it is clear that God calls people to repentance, but the lack of repentance is obvious in this story.

iii. *Is the main message that God goes to extraordinary lengths to try to recover a lost sheep?* I believe this is a secondary effect of the book, but yes. I believe that message secondarily comes through the book, but unfortunately the outcome does not model a happy ending, at least not yet.

iv. *Is it that God still talks to us through visions and dreams?* I believe this is a secondary effect of the book, but I do believe it is something that is necessary for the church and especially in the last days based off of Scripture.

v. *Is the main point that we should listen to God's voice and do whatever He asks?* I do believe this is a secondary effect of the book as well, maybe a 1-a purpose of the book. I know it is a strong emphasis throughout the book, and it models doing hard things for God—but I still believe it is a secondary effect.

vi. *Is the main point that we should listen to God's voice and do whatever He asks?* Yes, we should always obey God's voice, but it must *always* line up with Scripture and not contradict what the Word already says. And, we need to remember that obedience to what God asks us to do is the focus not the outcome. The outcome may not be what you would prefer, and you, like Job, may be confused for some time in your life, like I was. But, wait on the Lord, and in His time, He will fulfill this verse in your life: "Humble yourselves before the Lord, and he will exalt you" (James 4:10).

vii. *If the reader misses everything else, what is the one thing you want them to act on after reading this book?* God speaks to His children, and you can hear Him speak spiritually to you through reoccurring physical means—like the number *23* for me—to remind you He still *sees* you, He is *with* you, and He is *for* you.

7. **QUESTION: What if other believers never experience this type of 23 experience? Do you believe they are legitimate believers in Jesus Christ?**

ANSWER: Yes. I believe these are physical evidences of the spiritual presence of the Holy Spirit of God in one's life. But if this type of experience is not present, it does *not* mean you are not a believer in Jesus Christ. If you have placed your faith and trust in Jesus Christ as God in the flesh and the only way to eternal life, you are saved by God's grace for all of eternity. Romans 10:9-10 tells us,

> *Because, if you confess with your mouth that Jesus is Lord and believe in your heart that God raised him from the dead, you will be saved. For with the heart one believes and is justified, and with the mouth one confesses and is saved.*

If you have done this, you are a Christ follower, and heaven is your eternal home. The *23*s of this life are simply a means I find that God has used in my life, and potentially others, to remind them that He *still* sees them, and more importantly, He is *for* them.

8. **QUESTION: What do you mean by *mysticism*?**

ANSWER: I've used the word *mysticism* to mean "an immediate spiritual intuition of truths believed to transcend ordinary understanding or of a direct, intimate union of the soul with God through the Holy Spirit." I do not use the term as some secular, non-Christian interpreters do or within some Eastern religions. The Bible teaches us that the Holy Spirit lives within us and speaks to us and guides us. Jesus said, "my sheep hear my voice and know me." In a real sense, the Holy Spirit is our teacher and guide—helping us to be able to understand Scripture and God's living Word.

9. **QUESTION: What do you mean by *prophetic*? That sounds like you are trying to say you are a prophet like Jeremiah or Samuel. What Scripture can you share to explain better what you mean?**

ANSWER: I'm simply saying that I have the gift of prophesy as described in Acts. It is a gift from God provided to me when I was born again. God says He gives each believer spiritual gifts like discernment, administration, giving, speaking in tongues, prophesy, and others. Not everyone in the church has the same spiritual gift or gifts. But together we have all the gifts we need to function effectively as the body of Christ. So one of my spiritual gifts is prophesy. And through this spiritual gift, God sometimes reveals things to me that I could not know except through this gift.

However, I do not hold myself up as anything other than a pastor and disciple of Jesus who is trying to use the talents and gifts He has given me to help the church and bring glory to Jesus. Paul taught us to keep these spiritual gifts in perspective and use them in an orderly and proper manner. Paul taught us that all these spiritual gifts will one day pass away when we are with the Lord face to face—everything except faith, hope, and love—and as he tells us, love is the greatest of all these. So while I'm thankful for my spiritual gifts, they must be kept in proper perspective. To learn more, read these Scriptures that I've found helpful on this topic: 1 Corinthians 12 and 14.

10. QUESTION: What do you mean when you say someone, like your daughter, is a "prophetess"? What Scripture can you share to demonstrate this point of view is biblical?

ANSWER:

> *And he gave the apostles,* the prophets, *the evangelists, the shepherds and teachers, to equip the saints for the work of ministry, for building up the body of Christ, until we all attain to the unity of the faith and of the knowledge of the Son of God, to mature manhood, to the measure of the stature of the fullness of Christ. (Ephesians 4:11-13, emphasis added)*

This passage establishes that prophets are still for today in the New Testament church. It is a role of importance alongside apostles, evangelists, and shepherds. Some would argue that this was just for the Old Testament, but the order of these roles seems to beg the question, Why would Paul put this after apostles if he is simply referring to prophets of the Old Testament?

We know in Acts that Agabus, during the time of the early church, was a prophet. According to Acts 11:27-28, he was one of a group of prophets who travelled from Jerusalem to Antioch. Agabus had received the gift of prophecy and predicted a severe famine which the author of Acts says occurred during the reign of the Roman Emperor Claudius.

There are other prophets in the New Testament who received the gift of prophecy and predicted things as well, but one example will suffice to illuminate the authenticity and legitimacy of the gift in the early church.

Now that we have established the role of prophet in the New Testament and the gift of prophecy as a functioning gift in the body of Christ, there is another question: Is this role just for men, or are women included in this gift as well in the New Testament?

> *And in the last days it shall be, God declares, that I will pour out my Spirit on all flesh, and your sons and your daughters shall prophesy, and your young men shall see visions, and your old men shall dream dreams. (Acts 2:17)*

This verse establishes women as exercising the gift of prophesy as well in the time of the church age. A prophetess is simply a woman who prophesies, and we see this lived out in the New Testament:

> *And there was* a prophetess, *Anna, the daughter of Phanuel, of the tribe of Asher. She was advanced in years, having lived with her husband seven years from when she was a virgin, and then as a widow until she was eighty-four. She did not depart from the temple, worshiping with fasting and prayer night and day. And coming up at that very hour she began to give thanks to God and to speak of him to all who were waiting for the redemption of Jerusalem. (Luke 2:36-38, emphasis added)*

We also see this lived out in the early church in Acts:

> *On the next day we departed and came to Caesarea, and we entered the house of Philip the evangelist, who was one of the seven, and stayed with him. He had* four un-married *daughters, who prophesied. (Acts 21:8, emphasis added)*

When I say my daughter is a "prophetess," I simply mean she exercises the gift of prophecy in similar ways as I do and in ways that people in the early church did. She experiences and knows things she couldn't know without God revealing it. These previous verses show this is a common practice of the New

Testament church and is something we are still to practice today. First Corinthians 11:4-5 establishes this as a practice we are to exercise in the church service given the context of 1 Corinthians 11:

> *Every man who prays or prophesies with his head covered dishonors his head, but every wife who prays or prophesies . . . (1 Corinthians 11:4-5)*

This is not a gift we should avoid or limit to one gender nor is it an exercise we should keep from our church services. It is an important gift needed in the body of Christ, and it is one that keeps us aware of the perils of this life while maintaining the holiness God asks and expects of His bride, the church. The holiness of the church matters more to Him than the "success" of it, and this gift—used properly—keeps us sensitive to the holiness of God and the impending perils that come from poor judgment. This gift should never contradict or replace the Word of God in churches; it should supplement and draw attention to the weighty matters we sometimes drift from in an attempt to make church plausible, comfortable, acceptable, and relevant to the world around us.

ABOUT THE AUTHOR

KELLY M. WILLIAMS grew up on a dairy farm in Kentucky. He is a graduate of Liberty University (B.S. 1993) and Dallas Theological Seminary (ThM 1996).

After completing seminary, Kelly and his wife, Tosha, became qualified as church planter apprentices with the Home Mission Board of the Southern Baptist Convention. They moved to Colorado Springs and started Vanguard Church in 1997. Vanguard quickly gained local media attention as well as national attention in media outlets such as *Time, The 700 Club, Christianity Today, The New York Times,* and *ABC World News Tonight.* It is now one of the largest SBC churches in the state of Colorado. They expanded to three locations in 2017.

Kelly has now served as the Senior Pastor of Vanguard for 21 years. They have seen 3280 people follow Christ in believer's baptism and have partnered to help plant 69 other churches through the Frontline Church Planting Center. The SBC declared Vanguard in 2014 to be one of the top 30 SBC churches in its size range regarding conversion rate.

Along the way, Kelly has spoken for the Billy Graham Evangelistic Association. He published *Real Marriage: Where Fantasy Meets Reality* with his wife Tosha in 2008. He published *Friend of Sinners: Taking Risks to Reach the Lost* in 2017.

In addition to being the husband of Tosha, and the Senior Pastor of Vanguard Church, Kelly is the proud father of five children: Anastasha 20, Christianna 18, Joshua 16, Annalarie 14, and Journey Grace 11. Their family lives on a small farm in Colorado Springs. Having grown up in Kentucky, Kelly still loves Kentucky Wildcats Basketball.